Our selection of the city's best places to eat, drink and experience:

- ◎ **Sights**
- ✖ **Eating**
- ⊖ **Drinking**
- ✪ **Entertainment**
- 🔒 **Shopping**

These symbols give you the vital information for each listing:

- ✆ Telephone Numbers
- ⊘ Opening Hours
- P Parking
- ⊝ Nonsmoking
- @ Internet Access
- ⊚ Wi-Fi Access
- ✔ Vegetarian Selection
- 🗎 English-Language Menu

- ⚑ Family-Friendly
- 🐾 Pet-Friendly
- 🚍 Bus
- ⛴ Ferry
- M Metro
- S Subway
- 🚋 Tram
- R Train

Find each listing quickly on maps for each neighbourhood:

Bar Hemingway

16 ⊖ Map p233, B2

Legend has it that Hemi[ngway him]self, wielding a machine [gun, came to lib]erate this timber-pan[elled, leather-cov]ered bar during [WWII. The house] showpiece is a [martini, cho]sen by Papa an[d the best in] town. Dress [...s.com; Hôtel Rit[z ...; ⊘6.30pm-2a[m...

Lonely Planet's

...[ver]y memorable. We've split the city into easy-to-navigate neighbourhoods and provided clear maps so you'll find your way around with ease. Our expert authors have searched out the best of the city: walks, food, nightlife and shopping, to name a few. Because you want to explore, our 'Local Life' pages will take you to some of the most exciting areas to experience the real Athens.

And of course you'll find all the practical tips you need for a smooth trip: itineraries for short visits, how to get around, and how much to tip the guy who serves you a drink at the end of a long day's exploration.

It's your guarantee of a really great experience.

Our Promise

You can trust our travel information because Lonely Planet authors visit the places we write about, each and every edition. We never accept freebies for positive coverage, so you can rely on us to tell it like it is.

QuickStart Guide 7

Explore Athens 21

Worth a Trip:

The Best of Athens 135

Athens' Best Walks

Athens' Best...

Survival Guide 157

QuickStart Guide

Welcome to Athens

From the iconic Acropolis rising majestically above the expanse of the city to modern art galleries, charming neighbourhood squares and lively bars, bustling Athens is a delightfully quirky clash of past and present, a city that confronts and surprises. Visitors are drawn by ancient monuments bathed in the famous light, but it's the city's infectious, creative vibe that enamours and enlivens.

Entrance to the Acropolis (p24)
COLIN DUTTON/SIME/4CORNERS ©

Athens
Top Sights

Acropolis (p24)

The greatest symbol of the glory of Ancient Greece, and a wonder of the world, the Acropolis (High City) rises spectacularly over Athens. Explore its magnificent Parthenon, the pinnacle of classical civilisation.

EDUCATION IMAGES/UIG/GETTY IMAGES

Acropolis Museum (p30)

Natural light cascades through the spacious galleries of the modern Acropolis Museum, illuminating the priceless treasures of the Acropolis. The museum's top-floor glass atrium presents the 161m-long Parthenon frieze in its entirety.

Ancient Agora (p40)

Follow in the footsteps of Socrates at the *agora*, the heart of ancient Athens' civic life and the birthplace of democracy. The Agora Museum bursts with unusual finds and the Temple of Hephaestus is exquisite.

National Archaeological Museum (p100)

Greece's pre-eminent museum houses the world's largest and finest collection of Greek antiquities. Priceless items date from the neolithic era (6800 BC) to the Cycladic, Mycenaean and classical periods.

Temple of Olympian Zeus (p90)

Greece's largest temple took over 700 years to build. Only a handful of its colossal columns remain, but they help conjure the former size of this still mighty site, dedicated to Zeus and completed by the Roman Emperor Hadrian.

Benaki Museum
(p76)

This excellent private museum shows the spectrum of Greece's historical and cultural development, and its fight for Independence. More than 20,000 pieces are displayed chronologically over four levels of a stunning neoclassical mansion.

Keramikos (p124)

The city's ancient necropolis and ceremonial entrance is home to the impressive Street of Tombs and a superb small museum illustrating the splendour with which the ancient Greeks honoured their dead.

Filopappou Hill
(p114)

The mythical battleground of Theseus and the Amazons is studded with ruins, has a charming Byzantine church and looks over the whole Attica basin, with superb views of the Acropolis.

Athens Local Life

Insider tips to help you find the real city

After visiting Athens' magnificent ancient wonders it's time to experience life in the city: we'll show you the way through the downtown hurly-burly to quiet shaded cafes and delightful neighbourhood squares, and guide you to Athenians' favourite dining haunts, shopping spots, galleries and top bars.

Exploring Monastiraki (p44)

▶ Bustling markets
▶ Favourite hang-outs

Monastiraki's antique-lined squares and packed pedestrian markets always draw Athenians, but a new breed of coffee shops, restaurants and bars have sprung up and attract a hip, young crowd. Spend the day exploring the traditional and the trendy, manoeuvering through chaos and charm, grit and ancient splendour.

Wandering Central Market (p56)

▶ Awesome people-watching
▶ Sensory extravaganzas

Athens' Central Market anchors a neighbourhood thrumming with activity and sensations. The market and its environs are an extravaganza of colours, scents and sounds comprising spice shops, tavernas, art galleries and the city's premier *rembetika* club.

Shopping Around Plaka (p60)

▶ Cool boutiques
▶ Top cocktails

Plaka – with its historic houses, Byzantine churches and winding, narrow lanes climbing the slopes of the Acropolis – is much more than a tourist mecca. We'll show you how to shop like a local then head into Syntagma to find the city's most up-and-coming bar district.

People-Watching in Kolonaki (p78)

▶ Thriving cafe scene
▶ Sizzling nightlife

Kolonaki is home to Athens' haut monde. Watch the world go by from its popular streetside cafes, top-notch contemporary art galleries, and favourite low-key tavernas. Then pick between a night watching a film under the stars or clubbing with the fashionable set. Or do both!

Neighbourhood Life in Exarhia (p104)

▶ Graffiti-covered streets
▶ Lively restaurants & bars

Beneath Exarhia's gritty facade is one of Athens' most vibrant, unconventional neighbourhoods.

Outdoor dining in Monastiraki (p51)

Brettos bar (p70) in Plaka

Creative graffiti shouts social messages, and low-key cafes around Plateia Exarhion show its gentler side. Explore its super, laid-back eateries and join its dynamic student nightlife.

A Night Out in Gazi (p126)

▶ Eclectic eateries
▶ Bars galore

Gazi is synonymous with partying. Join Athenians surging into the neighbourhood each night and follow the party from bar to bar. Make a night of it by dining at any of its array of eateries then exploring rooftop-terrace cocktail bars, the city's gay scene or its high-end nightclubs.

Other great places to experience the city like a local:

Kalnterimi (p67)

Kalamaki Kolonaki (p84)

Toy (p70)

City (p85)

Ariston (p68)

Kalipateira (p51)

Saturday Farmer's Market (p111)

Sunday Flea Market (p121)

Athens
Day Planner

Day One

☀ Start with an early-morning climb through Plaka's streets to the glorious **Acropolis** (p24), going early to beat the crowds and the heat. Then wind your way down through the **Ancient Agora** (p40), the centre of ancient Athens' civic life. Venture into the streets of Plaka and Monastiraki, passing by the **Roman Agora** (p48) with its unusual Tower of the Winds, before heading to Monastiraki's souvlaki hub to initiate yourself with a *gyro* at **Thanasis** (p52), or have an excellent meal at sweet **Café Avyssinia** (p51).

☀ Explore the **Monastiraki Flea Market** (p44) or shop for souvenirs in Plaka, then head to the **Acropolis Museum** (p30) to see the Parthenon masterpieces. If you didn't see them while you were at the Acropolis, visit the **Theatre of Dionysos** (p28) and **Odeon of Herodes Atticus** (p29).

☾ Dine under the floodlit Acropolis at **Filistron** (p119) or **Strofi** (p35), then head to the best bars in Monastiraki and Syntagma, such as **Tailor Made** (p45) on Plateia Agia Irini, **Faust** (p54) with its cabaret, or one of the multitude of venues near Plateia Karytsi, like **Gin Joint** (p61).

Day Two

☀ Watch the **changing of the guard** (p64) ceremony at Parliament in Plateia Syntagmatos as the *evzones* strut their high-kicking stuff. Then head to the **Benaki Museum** (p76) for its extensive collections tracing Greek culture over millennia. In summer, plan to lunch alfresco on its terrace overlooking the National Gardens; in winter, stay cosy inside the wrap-around windows.

☀ Stroll down through the **National Gardens** (p64) to the old **Panathenaic Stadium** (p94) and then to the **Temple of Olympian Zeus** (p90) and **Hadrian's Arch** (p91). Dedicate the afternoon to seeing Greece's most significant antiquities at the **National Archaeological Museum** (p100), then head to bohemian **Exarhia** (p104) for an early meal.

☾ Take the funicular railway up **Lykavittos Hill** (p83) at sunset for impressive panoramic views of Athens and have dinner in Kolonaki at **Oikeio** (p79) or one of its many other fine restaurants, followed by a nightcap at **Rock'n'Roll** (p79), **Mai Tai** (p79) or **City** (p85). Alternatively, make your way to Gazi to dine at one of its trendy tavernas, such as **Kanella** (p130), and sip terrace-top drinks at a popular hotspot like **Gazarte** (p127), before bar-hopping til dawn.

Short on time?
We've arranged Athens' must-sees into these day-by-day itineraries to make sure you see the very best of the city in the time you have available.

Day Three

☀ Wander the wild **Athens Central Market** (p57) and the teeming streets around it, and stock up on food and drink to take home – such as this year's olive oil. Then have lunch at an old-world taverna nearby: try **Diporto Agoras** (p57).

☀ Make your way towards Kolonaki for high-end window-shopping or people-watching at its trendy cafes, and then get another dose of culture at the **Museum of Cycladic Art** (p82), **Byzantine & Christian Museum** (p82), **National Museum of Contemporary Art** (p64), or **National Art Gallery** (p83) – all in the same general vicinity.

☾ Dine in the centre at **Tzitzikas & Mermingas** (p67) for *mezedhes*, or **Paradosiako** (p68) for straight-up Greek fare with flare, then watch a moon-lit movie at one of Athens' outdoor cinemas such as **Aigli Cinema** (p97), **Cine Paris** (p71) or **Thission** (p121). Or, catch live local music at a *rembetika* club in winter, like **Stoa Athanaton** (p57). If it's summer, check programs for festivals, small venues like **Half Note Jazz Club** (p97) or **Cafe Alavastron** (p97), or hit a music taverna in Plaka or Psyrri.

Day Four

☀ Use the morning to immerse yourself in the **Keramikos** (p124) site with its grand Street of Tombs and small museum full of masterpieces. Then meander over to **Museum of Islamic Art** (p129) for its superb collection spanning centuries. Lunch in Monastiraki at **Kuzina** (p51) or in Psyrri at **Ivis** (p52) or **Nikitas** (p51).

☀ Then, make the long walk or quick cab-ride to the **Benaki Museum Pireos Annexe** (p129) for the latest contemporary art in a cool industrial building. Or take a stroll along the **pedestrian promenade** (p36), climbing **Filopappou Hill** (p114) for the views, then winding back to the cafes around Thisio.

☾ Pick your last meal in town, and if it's one of the top spots, like **Spondi** (p95) or **Varoulko** (p130), make sure you've booked ahead. Also plan ahead and get tickets for the **Odeon of Herodes Atticus** (p28) or **Megaron Mousikis** (p151) to see one of the city's grand theatre and musical venues in action. Alternatively, swing into one of Athens' new trendsetting spaces that are equal part gallery, cafe, bar and theatre: **Taf** (p45), **Six DOGS** (p45), or **Bios** (p133). Or, if it's summer, make the adventurous detour off-map to Glyfada's beach bars.

Need to Know

For more information, see Survival Guide (p158)

Currency
Euro (€)

Language
Greek

Visas
Not required for citizens of the EU or Schengen countries; not required for stays up to 90 days for the US, Canada, Australia and New Zealand.

Money
ATMs widely available. Credit cards accepted in many hotels, restaurants and shops, but not all.

Mobile Phones
Local SIM cards can be used in European and Australian phones. Most other phones can be set to roaming. US/Canadian phones need to have a dual or tri-band system.

Time
Eastern European Time (GMT/UTC plus two hours, or plus three hours during daylight savings).

Plugs & Adaptors
Plugs have two round pins; electrical current is 220-240V. North American visitors will require an adaptor and a transformer.

Tipping
Small change and rounding up is usually sufficient.

 Before You Go

Your Daily Budget

Budget less than €100
► Dorm beds €25, pension doubles from €65
► Souvlaki shops and tavernas are good value
► Stretch your euros in the low season

Midrange €100-€200
► Double rooms in midrange hotels €80-€160
► Local tavernas have hearty midrange fare
► Most sights have reasonable entrance fees

Top End more than €200
► Double rooms in top hotels from €150
► Excellent dining; some accompanied by Michelin stars
► Nightlife and cocktail bars abound

Useful Websites

Athens' Official Site (www.breathtaking athens.gr) With what's-on listings.

Ministry of Culture (www.culture.gr) Museums and archaeological sites.

Lonely Planet (www.lonelyplanet.com/ Greece/Athens) Information, hotel bookings, traveller forum.

Advance Planning

Three months before Reserve your hotel early to increase choice and reduce price.

One month before Book tickets for a performance at Odeon of Herodes Atticus or Megaron Mousikis. Reserve a table at top-end restaurants.

One week before Check online for strike information (http://livingingreece.gr/ strikes); book tours.

2 Arriving in Athens

Most visitors arrive at Athens' Eleftherios Venizelos International Airport at Spata, 27km east of the city centre. Most ferries and cruises arrive at the port of Piraeus.

✈ From Eleftherios Venizelos International Airport

Destination	Best Transport
Syntagma & Plaka	Metro (blue line)
	Express bus X95
Monastiraki	Metro (blue line)
Thisio	Metro (blue line to green line)
Kolonaki	Metro (blue line)
	Express bus X95
Makrygianni	Metro (blue line to red line)
Psyrri	Metro (blue line)

⚓ From Piraeus Port

Destination	Best Transport
Syntagma & Plaka	Metro (green line to blue line)
	Bus 040
Monastiraki	Metro (green line)
Thisio	Metro (green line)
Kolonaki	Metro (green line to blue line)
Makrygianni	Metro (green line to red line)
Psyrri	Metro (green line)

✈ At the Airport

Eleftherios Venizelos International Airport
The arrivals hall has ATMs, tourist information, car hire and baggage storage. For those who need to sleep out by the airport to catch an early flight, there are only two hotels: Sofitel, right at the terminal, and Holiday Inn, a 15-minute shuttle ride away.

3 Getting Around

Athens has an extensive and inexpensive integrated public transport network of buses, metro, trolleybuses and trams. Pick up maps and timetables at the EOT tourist office, the airport, or online at www.oasa. gr. The metro (www.amel.gr) is the best way to get around town. Conveniently, all public transport operates under the same ticketing system. Tickets good for 90 minutes (€1.40), a 24-hour travel pass (€4) and a weekly ticket (€14) are valid for all forms of public transport except for airport services (airport metro €8, bus €5).

M Metro

Three colour-coded lines criss-cross central Athens. Line 1 (green) also serves Piraeus. Line 2 (red) gets the closest to the Acropolis and the Acropolis Museum. Line 3 (blue) serves the airport. The central hubs are Syntagma (blue and red lines) and Monastiraki (blue and green lines).

🚌 Bus, Trolleybus & Tram

Blue-and-white local express buses, regular buses and electric trolleybuses operate every 15 minutes from 5am to midnight. They are generally slower than the metro, and best for neighbourhoods outside the centre. The free OASA map shows most routes. Athens' tram (www.tramsa.gr) offers a slow, scenic coastal journey to Faliro and Voula, via Glyfada.

🚕 Taxi

Avoid driving in Athens at all costs – it is much simpler and cheaper to take a cab, but beware of taxi driver scams (p163).

Athens
Neighbourhoods

Ancient Agora, Monastiraki & Psyrri (p38)
The ancient Athenian civic centre spills into the modern city's central shopping hub – a heady mix of eclectic shops, restaurants and bars.

◉ Top Sights

Ancient Agora

Keramikos & Gazi (p122)
The city's ancient cemetery, Keramikos, leads to the illuminated towers of Gazi's Technopolis and the hottest bar district in Athens.

◉ Top Sights

Keramikos

Filopappou Hill & Thisio (p112)
Unwind in the quiet stretch of town spanning ruin-strewn Filopappou Hill and the cafe-lined pedestrianised streets of cool Thisio.

◉ Top Sights

Filopappou Hill

Acropolis Area (p22)
Explore the grand Acropolis and the superb Acropolis Museum, then wander the relatively quiet streets of Makrygianni.

◉ Top Sights

Acropolis

Acropolis Museum

Keramikos

Ancient Agora

Acropolis

Acropolis Museum

Filopappou Hill

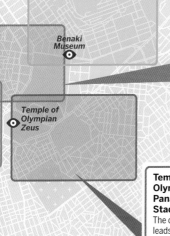

National Archaeological Museum & Exarhia (p98)

Discover the treasures at the world's foremost collection of Greek art and antiquities, then soak up the vibe in bohemian Exarhia.

◉ Top Sights

National Archaeological Museum

Benaki Museum & Kolonaki (p74)

Consistently fashionable and loaded with popular boutiques, cafes and bars, Kolonaki is also home to some of the city's premier museums, including the Benaki.

◉ Top Sights

Benaki Museum

Greek Parliament, Syntagma & Plaka (p58)

Parliament anchors enormous Plateia Syntagmatos, and the winding lanes of Plaka, lined with shops, become quaintly residential as they twist up the slope of the Acropolis.

Temple of Olympian Zeus & Panathenaic Stadium (p88)

The colossal temple leads to the stadium, the home of the first modern Olympic games, and laid-back residential neighbourhoods Mets and Pangrati.

◉ Top Sights

Temple of Olympian Zeus

National Archaeological Museum

Benaki Museum

Temple of Olympian Zeus

Explore
Athens

Gate of Athena Archegetis, Roman Agora (p48)
DENNIS K JOHNSON/GETTY IMAGES ©

Explore

Acropolis Area

Athens' crown jewel is, of course, the Acropolis. This epic monument stands sentinel over the city, and on its southern slopes a fabulous modern museum holds its treasures in spacious splendour. The pedestrian promenade between the Acropolis and the Acropolis Museum bustles with tourists, and despite being just south of this historic hub the quiet neighbourhood of Makrygianni is refreshingly untouristy.

The Sights in a Day

☀️ Start as early as you can manage to make your way to the Acropolis and beat the heat and the crowds. Wander the hilltop first, from the **Parthenon** (p25) to the resplendent **Caryatids** (p31) at the **Erechtheion** (p26) and the precious **Temple of Athena Nike** (p28). Wander down the Acropolis' southern slope to take in the **Odeon of Herodes Atticus** (p29), the **Stoa of Eumenes** (p28) and the **Theatre of Dionysos** (p28).

🌤️ Grab a bite to eat at the superscenic and relaxing **Acropolis Museum** (p30) cafe-restaurant before taking plenty of time to peruse the thousands of works in the collection. You can examine everything from tiny coins to magnificent pedimental sculptures, all arrayed beautifully in the modern (air-conditioned!) building. The movie on the top floor makes a nice break, too.

🌙 If there's any time left before dinner, check out neighbourhood shops, including **El.Marneri Galerie** (p36), **Greece is For Lovers** (p37) and **Kanakis** (p37), or take a short stroll along the **Ancient Promenade** (p36), listening to the buskers. Plan to dine out at one of the area's fine restaurants, such as **Mani Mani** (p35), **Strofi** (p35) or **Dionysos** (p35) and then hit **Duende** (p36) or **Tiki Athens** (p36) for a nightcap.

👁️ Top Sights

Acropolis (p24)

Acropolis Museum (p30)

🖤 Best of Athens

Archaeological Sites

Acropolis (p24)

Theatre of Dionysos (p28)

Odeon of Herodus Atticus (p29)

Museums

Acropolis Museum (p30)

Food

Mani Mani (p35)

Getting There

Ⓜ **Metro** The metro is the best option. Akropoli station (red line) sits near the Acropolis Museum at the base of the Acropolis hill, just off the major boulevard Leoforos Syngrou.

Ⓜ **Metro** Arriving at Syntagma station (blue and red lines) or Monastiraki station (blue and green lines), to the west of the Acropolis hill, allows for a leisurely walk through Plaka's winding lanes to the Acropolis' western entrance.

Top Sights
Acropolis

The Acropolis is the most important ancient site in the Western world. Crowned by the Parthenon, it rises over Athens, visible from almost everywhere within the city. Its monuments of Pentelic marble gleam white in the midday sun and gradually take on a honey hue as the sun sinks, while at night they stand brilliantly illuminated above the city. A glimpse of this magnificent sight cannot fail to exalt your spirit.

◉ Map p32, B2

☎ 210 321 0219

http://odysseus.culture.gr

adult/child €12/6

🕗 8am-8pm Mon-Fri, to 3pm Sat & Sun

Ⓜ Akropoli

Parthenon

Don't Miss

Parthenon

The Parthenon is the monument that more than any other epitomises the glory of Ancient Greece. It is dedicated to Athena Parthenos, the goddess embodying the power and prestige of the city. The largest Doric temple ever completed in Greece, and the only one built completely of Pentelic marble (apart from the wood in its roof), it was designed by Iktinos and Kallicrates to be the pre-eminent monument of the Acropolis and was completed in time for the Great Panathenaic Festival of 438 BC.

Parthenon Columns

The Parthenon's fluted Doric columns achieve perfect form. The eight columns at either end and 17 on each side were ingeniously curved to create an optical illusion: the foundations (like all the 'horizontal' surfaces of the temple) are slightly concave and the columns are slightly convex making both appear straight. Supervised by Pheidias, the sculptors Agoracritos and Alcamenes worked on the architectural sculptures of the Parthenon, including the pediments, frieze and metopes, which were brightly coloured and gilded.

Parthenon Pediments

The temple's pediments (the triangular elements topping the east and west facades) were filled with elaborately carved three-dimensional sculptures. The west side depicted Athena and Poseidon in their contest for the city's patronage, the east Athena's birth from Zeus' head. See their remnants and the rest of the Acropolis' sculptures and artefacts in the Acropolis Museum.

☑ Top Tips

▶ Visit early in the morning to escape crowds and searing afternoon heat.

▶ The main entrance is from Dionysiou Areopagitou near the Odeon of Herodes Atticus; budget cuts have reduced opening hours of some of the other entrances.

▶ Wheelchairs access the site via a cage lift; go to the main entrance.

▶ Large bags must be left at the main entrance cloakroom.

▶ Sundays between November and March are free.

▶ Acropolis admission includes entry to other sites (p35).

✕ Take a Break

Swing into Dionysos (p35) for coffee and excellent views of the monument.

Or, book ahead for a late afternoon lunch at Mani Mani (p35), where regional Peloponnesian cuisine is featured.

JEAN-PIERRE LESCOURRET/GETTY IMAGES ©

The Metopes & Frieze

The Parthenon's metopes, designed by Pheidias, are square carved panels set between channelled triglyphs. The metopes on the eastern side depicted the Olympian gods fighting the giants, and on the western side they showed Theseus leading the Athenian youths into battle against the Amazons. The southern metopes illustrated the contest of the Lapiths and Centaurs at a marriage feast, while the northern ones depicted the sacking of Troy. The internal cella was topped by the Ionic frieze, a continuous sculptured band depicting the Panathenaic Procession.

The Original Statue: Athena Polias

The statue for which the temple was built – the Athena Polias (Athena of the City) – was considered one of the wonders of the ancient world. It was taken to Constantinople in AD 426, where it disappeared. Designed by Pheidias and completed in 432 BC, it stood almost 12m high on its pedestal and was plated in gold. Athena's face, hands and feet were made of ivory, and the eyes fashioned from jewels.

Erechtheion

The Erechtheion, completed around 406 BC, was a sanctuary built on the part of the Acropolis held most sacred: the spot where Poseidon struck the ground with his trident, and where Athena produced the olive tree. Named after Erechtheus, a mythical king of Athens, the temple housed the cults of Athena, Poseidon and Erechtheus. This

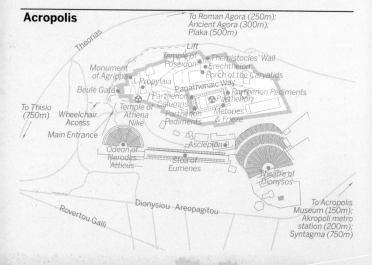

Acropolis

To Roman Agora (250m);
Ancient Agora (300m);
Plaka (500m)

Theorias

Lift

Temple of Poseidon

Themistocles' Wall

Monument of Agrippa

Erechtheion

Propylaia

Porch of the Caryatids

Beulé Gate

Panathenaic Way

Parthenon Pediments

To Thisio (750m)

Wheelchair Access

Temple of Athena Nike

Parthenon Columns

Parthenon

Parthenon Pediments

Metopes & Frieze

Main Entrance

Odeon of Herodes Atticus

Asclepion

Stoa of Eumenes

Theatre of Dionysos

Dionysiou Areopagitou

To Acropolis Museum (150m); Akropoli metro station (200m); Syntagma (750m)

Rovertou Galli

Caryatids of the Erechtheion

supreme example of Ionic architecture was ingeniously built on several levels to counteract the uneven bedrock.

Porch of the Caryatids

The Erechtheion is immediately recognisable by the six majestic maiden columns that support its southern portico, the Caryatids (415 BC). Modelled on women from Karyai (modern-day Karyes, in Lakonia), each maiden is thought to have held a libation bowl in one hand, and to be drawing up her dress with the other. Those you see are plaster casts. The originals (except for one removed by Lord Elgin, now in the British Museum) are in the Acropolis Museum.

Temple of Poseidon

Though he didn't win patronage of the city, Poseidon was worshipped on the northern side of the Erechtheion. The porch still bears the mark of his trident-strike. Imagine the finely decorated coffered porch painted in rich colours, as it was before.

Themistocles' Wall

Crafty general Themistocles (524–459 BC) hastened to build a protective wall around the Acropolis and in so doing incorporated elements from archaic temples on the site. Look for the column drums built into the wall on the north side of the Erechtheion.

Propylaia

The monumental entrance to the Acropolis, the Propylaia was built by Mnesicles between 437 BC and 432 BC and consists of a central hall with two wings on either side. In ancient times its five gates were the only entrances to the 'upper city'. The middle gate opens onto the **Panathenaic Way**. The ceiling of the central hall was painted with gold stars on a dark-blue background.

Temple of Athena Nike

Recently restored, this exquisitely proportioned tiny Pentelic marble temple was designed by Kallicrates and built around 425 BC. The internal cella housed a wooden statue of Athena as Victory (Nike) and the exterior friezes illustrated scenes from mythology, the Battle of Plataea (479 BC) and Athenians fighting Boeotians and Persians.

Beulé Gate & Monument of Agrippa

Just outside of the Propylaia lies the Beulé Gate, named after French archaeologist Ernest Beulé, who uncovered it in 1852. The 8m pedestal halfway up the zigzagging ramp to the Propylaia was once topped by the Monument of Agrippa. This bronze statue of the Roman general riding a chariot was erected in 27 BC to commemorate victory in the Panathenaic Games (p43).

Theatre of Dionysos

Originally, a 6th-century-BC timber theatre was built here, on the site of the Festival of the Great Dionysia (p34). During Athens' golden age, the theatre hosted productions of the works of Aeschylus, Sophocles, Euripides and Aristophanes. Reconstructed in stone and marble between 342 and 326 BC, the theatre held 17,000 spectators (spread over 64 tiers, of which only about 20 tiers survive) and an altar to Dionysos in the orchestra pit.

Theatre of Dionysos Thrones & Carvings

The ringside Pentelic marble thrones were for dignitaries and priests. The grandest, with lions' paws, satyrs and griffins, was reserved for the Priest of Dionysos. The reliefs at the rear of the stage depict the exploits of Dionysos.

Asclepion & Stoa of Eumenes

Above the Theatre of Dionysos, steps lead to the Asclepion, a temple built around a sacred spring. The worship of Asclepius, the physician son of Apollo, began in Epidavros and was introduced to Athens in 429 BC at a time when plague was sweeping the city: people sought cures here.

Beneath the Asclepion, the Stoa of Eumenes is a colonnade built by Eumenes II, King of Pergamum (197–159 BC).

Odeon of Herodes Atticus

The path continues west from the Asclepion to the magnificent **Odeon of Herodes Atticus**. It was built in AD 161 by wealthy Roman Herodes Atticus in memory of his wife Regilla. Performances of drama, music and dance are held here during the **Athens Festival** (☎ 210 322 1459; www.hellenicfestival.gr).

Understand

The Acropolis

- -

Contest for Athens

After Kekrops, a Phoenician, founded a city on a huge rock near the sea, the gods of Olympus proclaimed that it should be named after the deity who could provide the most valuable legacy for mortals. Athena (goddess of wisdom, among other things) produced an olive tree, symbol of peace and prosperity. Poseidon (god of the sea) struck a rock with his trident and a saltwater spring emerged (some versions of the myth say he made a horse). The gods judged that Athena's gift would better serve the citizens of Athens with nourishment, oil and wood. To this day the goddess dominates Athens' mythology and the city's great monuments are dedicated to her.

Building the Acropolis

The Acropolis was first inhabited in neolithic times (4000–3000 BC). The first temples were built during the Mycenaean era in homage to the goddess Athena. People lived on the Acropolis until the late 6th century BC, but in 510 BC the Delphic Oracle declared that it should be the province of the gods.

After all the buildings on the Acropolis were reduced to ashes by the Persians on the eve of the Battle of Salamis (480 BC), Pericles set about his ambitious rebuilding program. He transformed the Acropolis into a city of temples, now regarded as the zenith of classical Greek achievement. He spared no expense: only the best materials, architects, sculptors – such as Pheidias – and artists were good enough for a city dedicated to the cult of Athena. The city was a showcase of lavishly coloured colossal buildings and of gargantuan statues, some of bronze, others of marble plated with gold and encrusted with precious stones.

Preserving the Site

The temples have suffered through the years of foreign occupation, pilfering by foreign archaeologists, inept renovations following Independence, earthquakes and, most recently, acid rain and pollution. The worst damage occurred in 1687 when the Venetians attacked the Turks, opening fire on the Acropolis and causing an explosion in the Parthenon, where the Turks were storing gunpowder. Major restoration programs are ongoing.

Top Sights
Acropolis Museum

The grand modernist Acropolis Museum at the southern foot of the Acropolis displays the monument's surviving treasures. While the collection covers the Archaic and Roman periods, the emphasis is on the Acropolis of the 5th century BC, considered the apotheosis of Greece's artistic achievement. The spectacular museum cleverly showcases layers of history: subterranean ruins are visible below, and the Acropolis rises above, thus allowing visitors to see the masterpieces in context.

⊙ Map p32, C4

www.theacropolismuseum.gr

Dionysiou Areopagitou 15, Makrygianni

admission €5

⊙8am-8pm Tue-Sun, to 10pm Fri

Ⓜ Akropoli

Acropolis Museum

Don't Miss

Archaic Gallery

Bathed in natural light, the 1st floor is a veritable forest of statues, mostly offerings to Athena. These include stunning examples of 6th-century *kore* (maiden) statues: young women in draped clothing and elaborate braids.

Early Temple Treasures

The Archaic Gallery also houses bronze figurines and finds from temples predating the Parthenon which were destroyed by the Persians. Elaborate pedimental sculptures include Heracles slaying the Lernaian Hydra and a lioness devouring a bull.

Parthenon Gallery

The museum's crowning glory, this top-floor glass atrium built in alignment with the Parthenon showcases the Parthenon's pediments, metopes and 160m frieze. For the first time in over 200 years, the frieze is displayed in sequence, depicting the Panathenaic Procession. Interspersed between golden-hued originals are white plaster replicas of missing pieces (the controversial Parthenon Marbles taken by Lord Elgin in 1801).

Caryatids

Five grand Caryatids, the world-famous maiden columns that held up the porch of the Erechtheion, rule the mezzanine (the sixth is in the British Museum). Nearby, find a giant floral *akrotirion* (decorative element at the end of a gable of a classical building) that once crowned the southern ridge of the Parthenon pediment.

Foyer Gallery

Finds from the slopes of the Acropolis fill the entryway gallery, while the glass floor allows glimpses of the ruins below.

☑ Top Tips

▶ Beneath the entrance look for the ruins of an ancient Athenian neighbourhood which have been cleverly incorporated into the museum design after being uncovered during excavations.

▶ Leave time for the movie describing the history of the Acropolis (top floor) and the fine museum shop (ground floor).

▶ Last admission is a half-hour before closing, and galleries are cleared 15 minutes before closing.

▶ Bring ID if you are under 18 or a student for free admission. EU citizens who are over 65 are also free with ID.

✗ Take a Break

The museum's cafe-restaurant on the second floor has superb views across the way to the Acropolis, and prices are surprisingly reasonable (mains €10 to €15). Eat inside or sip a coffee alfresco on the terrace.

A   B   C   D

Mitroou

Thrasyvoulou

Tholou

Aretousas

Areopagus
Hill

1

Theorias

Prytaniou

ANAFIOTIKA

0   200 m
0   0.1 miles

Sholiou

Adrianou

Kekropos

Tripodon

Rangava

Kydathineon

Plateia
Filomousou
Eterias

Afroditis

Adrianou

Herefontos

Goura

◉ *Acropolis*

Stratonos

Thespidos

Epimenidou

Lysikratous

Frynihou

Eschinou

2

Entrance

Thrasyllou

Vakhou

Theorias

Entrance to Theatre of
Dionysos & Acropolis ●

Vyronos

Vyronos

Grand Promenade

Dionysiou Areopagitou

🅸

🅸

◀◉ 5

3

Webster

Ilias Lalaounis
Jewellery Museum **1** ◉

Kallisperi

Karyatidon

Mitseon

MAKRYGIANNI

Ⓜ
Akropoli

Makri

Ⓟ
7

2 ◉ ⊗
4

Atelier Spyros
Vassiliou

Propyleon

Fratti

Rovertou Galli

Ⓜ
Porinou

Diakou Ath

13
🔒

Angelikara

Promahou

*Acropolis
Museum* ◉

11 🔒
Lembesi

Kaleshrou

⊗ **6**

Garivaldi

Kavalloti

🔒 **12**

Hatzihristou

Ⓟ **10**

4

Drakou

Erehthiou

Parthenos

Petmeza

Zitrou

Mitromara

Strateon

Plateia
Tsokri

Vourvahi

Koryzi

Nezer Th

Tsami Karatasi

Ⓟ
9

 Filinon

Ⓟ
8

Negri Th

Nakou

Petmeza

Veikou

⊗ **3**

Stratigou Kondouli

Dimitrakopoulou N

Falirou

Leof Syngrou Andrea

Donda Sp

Kallirrois

Sights

Ilias Lalaounis Jewellery Museum

MUSEUM

1 ◉ Map p32, B3

Jewellery and decorative arts inspired by Greek history showcase the talents of Greece's renowned jeweller Ilias Lalaounis. The museum demonstrates jewellery-making techniques from prehistoric times. The permanent collection includes displays of more than 4000 pieces of jewellery and intricate microsculptures designed by Lalaounis since the 1940s. (☏ 210 922 1044; www. lalaounis-jewelrymuseum.gr; Kallisperi 12, cnr Karyatidon, Makrygianni; admission €5, free Sat; ⏰ 9am-4pm Mon & Thu-Sat, to 9pm Wed, 11am-4pm Sun; Ⓜ Akropoli)

Atelier Spyros Vassiliou

ART GALLERY

2 ◉ Map p32, A3

The home and studio of leading 20th-century Greek painter and set designer Spyros Vassiliou (1902–1985) has been converted into an impressive museum and archive of his work. Exhibits include his celebrated paintings depicting urban Athens, theatre sets, his artist's tools and illustrations from literary journals and newspapers. (☏ 210 923 1502; www.spyrosvassiliou.org; Webster 5a, Makrygianni; adult/child €4/2;

GEORGE TSAFOS/GETTY IMAGES ©

Dining at Strofi (p35), below the Acropolis

Understand

Birthplace of Theatre

The tyrant Peisistratos introduced the annual Festival of the Great Dionysia during the 6th century BC, and held it in the world's first theatre on the south slope of the Acropolis. During the festival masses of people attended contests where men clad in goatskins sang and danced, followed by feasting and revelry. Drama as we know it dates back to these contests. At one of them, Thespis left the ensemble and took centre stage for a solo performance, an act considered to be the first true dramatic performance – hence the term 'thespian'.

Drama in the Golden Age

During the golden age in the 5th century BC, the festival was one of the state's major events. Politicians sponsored dramas by writers such as Aeschylus, Sophocles and Euripides, with lighter relief provided by the bawdy comedies of Aristophanes. People came from all over Attica, with their expenses met by the state.

In Roman times, the theatre was also used for performances and state events.

Greek Theatre Today

The works of the ancient Greek playwrights, as well as more 'modern' plays and operas, are still performed in the few surviving ancient theatres during summer festivals, like the Hellenic Festival (www.greekfestival. gr; ☺late May–Oct). The most notable of these are the Odeon of Herodes Atticus and the stunningly preserved theatre in Epidavros in the Peloponnese.

Athens also supports a lively winter theatre tradition, with more than 200 theatres (more than any other European city) presenting anything from Sophocles to Becket and works by contemporary Greek playwrights. The Megaron Mousikis (p151) is the modern symphony hall, and the National Theatre is in the Omonia neighbourhood.

🕐10am-4pm Tue, Fri & Sat, noon-6pm Wed, 10am-2pm Sun, closed mid-Aug; Ⓜ Akropoli)

before 7pm, allowing you to try a range of dishes. (📞210 921 8180; www.manimani. com.gr; Falirou 10, Makrygianni; mains €9.50-16; 🕐3pm-12.30am Tue-Thu, from 1pm Fri & Sat, 1-5.30pm Sun, closed Jul & Aug; Ⓜ Akropoli)

Eating

Mani Mani   FINE DINING €€

3 Map p32, C5

In a welcoming setting on the 1st floor of a charming neoclassical building, this delightful modern restaurant specialises in regional cuisine from Mani in the Peloponnese. The ravioli with Swiss chard, chervil and cheese, and the tangy Mani sausage with orange, are standouts. It's great value and almost all starters and mains can be ordered as half serves (at half price)

Strofi   FINE DINING €

4 Map p32, A3

Book ahead here for a Parthenon view from the rooftop of this exquisitely renovated townhouse. Food is simple Greek, but the setting with elegant white linen, burgundy walls, original art and sweet service elevates the experience to romantic levels. (📞210 921 4130; www.strofi.gr; Rovertou Galli 25, Makrygianni; mains €11-15; Ⓜ Akropoli)

Dionysos   FINE DINING, CAFE €€

5 Map p32, A3

Location, location, location. Eat here for the fantastic sweep of plate glass looking out onto the unblemished south slope of the Acropolis. Food is pricey but service is attentive...Date night? Or pop in for a coffee break. (📞210 923 1939; www.dionysoszonars.gr; Rovertou Galli 43, Makrygianni; mains €18-28; 🕐restaurant noon-1am, cafe 8am-1am; Ⓜ Akropoli)

Aglio, Olio & Peperoncino   ITALIAN €€

6 Map p32, D4

Hardly the most obvious or inviting place for a restaurant, but this hidden gem behind the metro is a great choice for no-frills classic Italian cuisine, good-value pastas

---

☑️ Top Tip

Six for the Price of One

The €12 Acropolis admission includes entry to Athens' main ancient sites: Ancient Agora, Roman Agora, Keramikos, the Temple of Olympian Zeus and the Theatre of Dionysos. The ticket is valid for four days; otherwise individual site fees apply (though this is not strictly enforced). Usually, similar opening hours (8am to 8pm April to October, 8.30am to 3pm November to March) apply for all of these sites, but it pays to double-check as hours fluctuate from year to year. Enter the sites free on the first Sunday of the month (except for July, August and September) and on certain holidays.

with authentic Italian flavours and a cosy, trattoria ambience. (📞210 921 1801; Porinou 13, Makrygianni; mains €15-25; ⏱noon-midnight Mon-Fri, 8pm-2am Sat, 2-7pm Sun; Ⓜ Akropoli)

Drinking

Duende

BAR

7 🍷 Map p32, D3

An established local haunt, this intimate French brasserie–style bar with sedate music and a mature crowd is ideal for a quiet meal or drink at the bar. (Tziraion 2, Makrygianni; Ⓜ Akropoli)

Local Life
Ancient Promenade

The once traffic-choked streets around Athens' historic centre were transformed into a spectacular 3km pedestrian promenade connecting the city's most significant ancient sites. In the evenings, locals and tourists alike come out in force for an evening *volta* (walk) along the stunning cobblestone boulevard – one of Europe's longest pedestrian precincts – under the floodlit Acropolis.

The **grand promenade** starts at Dionysiou Areopagitou, opposite the Temple of Olympian Zeus, and continues along the southern foothills of the Acropolis, all the way to the Ancient Agora, branching off from Thisio to Keramikos and Gazi, and north along Adrianou to Monastiraki and Plaka.

Tiki Athens

BAR, RESTAURANT

8 🍷 Map p32, C4

Funky '50s decor, an Asian-inspired menu, plus burgers, and an alternative hip, young crowd make this a fun place for a drink. Sample the impressive cocktail list to eclectic sounds ranging from jazz and rockabilly to Tom Waits. (📞210 923 6908; www.tikiathens.com; Falirou 15, Makrygianni; ⏱4.30pm-late; Ⓜ Akropoli)

Sports Club

BAR, RESTAURANT

9 🍷 Map p32, C4

Americanos, Americanos, Americanos! You'll find a solid collection of them here at this efficiently run bar. There's also breakfast and pub food like fish and chips. (Veikou 3a, Makrygianni; Ⓜ Akropoli)

Lamda Club

GAY BAR

10 🍷 Map p32, D4

Despite the gay scene drifting to Gazi, this three-level gay club is still one of the busiest in Athens, and not for the faint of heart, with a diverse late-night crowd. Pop, house and Greek music dominate, with two basement-dark rooms. (📞210 942 4202; Lembesi 15, cnr Leoforos Syngrou; Ⓜ Akropoli)

Shopping

El.Marneri Galerie

JEWELLERY, ART

11 🔒 Map p32, D4

Sample rotating exhibitions of local modern art and some of the best

Theatre of Dionysos (p28) and Acropolis Museum (p30)

jewellery in the city, like that made by Astarti. Handmade, unusual, and totally eye-catching. (☎210 861 9488; www.elenimarneri.com; Lembesi 5-7, Makrygianni; ☉10am-8pm Tue, Thu & Fri, to 6pm Wed & Sat; Ⓜ Akropoli)

Greece Is For Lovers
SOUVENIRS

12 🔒 Map p32, B4

Browse the cheeky designer plays on Greek kitsch: from Corinthian column dumb-bells to crocheted iPod covers. Look for the giant Grecian sandal skateboard in the window. (☎210 924 5064; www.greeceisforlovers.com; Karyatidon 13a, Makrygianni; Ⓜ Akropoli)

Kanakis
JEWELLERY

13 🔒 Map p32, D4

Contemporary jewellery from Cretan Spiros Kanakis, who often plays on ancient Greek motifs in his original gold designs; mostly handmade in his Iraklio workshop. (☎210 922 8297; Stratigou Makrygianni 17, Makrygianni; Ⓜ Akropoli)

Explore

Ancient Agora, Monastiraki & Psyrri

Busy Monastiraki's central square opens onto its packed flea market, a warren of antique shops and great people-watching. To the south, the Ancient Agora was the city's original civic meeting place and remains a wonderful site to explore. Just north of Monastiraki lies Psyrri, where dilapidated facades belie the lively quarter where restaurants and bars coexist with an offbeat mix of warehouse conversions and workshops.

The Sights in a Day

☀ Start the day wandering the **Ancient Agora** (p40) and examining the priceless artefacts in its excellent museum housed in the Stoa of Attalos. If time permits, check out the elaborately carved **Tower of the Winds** (p48) at the **Roman Agora** (p48).

☀ Break for lunch along Adrianou at **Kuzina** (p51) or another of the plethora of cafes and restaurants, or find your way to **Café Avyssinia** (p51) for Acropolis views and old-world elegance. Then cruise the **Monastiraki flea market** and shop for souvenirs in its wild array of shops. Or swing into **Spiliopoulos** (p55) for discount designer duds and **Melissinos Art** (p55) for handcrafted sandals.

☾ Wrap up your day at **Magaze** (p52) for pre-dinner cocktails, then choose between haute cuisine at **Hytra** (p51) or savoury street fare at **Thanasis** (p52). As it nears midnight, make your way to **Faust** (p54) or other area clubs to dance the night away.

For a local's day in Monastiraki, see p44.

👁 Top Sights
Ancient Agora (p40)

🔍 Local Life
Exploring Monastiraki (p44)

💜 Best of Athens
Food
Cafe Avyssinia (p51)

Hytra (p51)

Mama Roux (p45)

Kostas (p45)

Thanasis (p52)

Shopping
Monastiraki Flea Market (p44)

Mompso (p45)

Martinos (p54)

Spiliopoulos (p55)

Melissinos Art (p55)

Sabater Hermanos (p55)

Getting There

Ⓜ **Metro** The Monastiraki station (blue and green lines) sits at the edge of the flea market and the Ancient and Roman Agoras are a short walk south.

Ⓜ **Metro** The Thisio station (green line) is just west of Monastiraki, and also offers easy access. Psyrri is north of both stations.

Top Sights
Ancient Agora

The heart of ancient Athens was the 6th-century BC Agora, the lively focal point of administrative, commercial, political and social activity. Socrates expounded his philosophy here, and in AD 49 St Paul came here to win converts to Christianity. Devastated by the Persians in 480 BC, it was rebuilt and flourished through Pericles' time and until AD 267, when it was destroyed by the Herulians. The Turks built a residential quarter here, but archaeologists demolished it after Independence and later excavated to classical and, in parts, neolithic levels.

👁 ☎ 210 321 0185

http://odysseus.culture.gr

Adrianou

adult/child €4/2, with Acropolis pass free

🕗8am-3pm, museum closed 8-11am Mon

Ⓜ Monastiraki

Temple of Hephaestus (p42), Ancient Agora

Don't Miss

Stoa of Attalos

A stoa is a covered walkway or portico, and the grand Stoa of Attalos served as the first-ever shopping arcade. Built by namesake King Attalos II of Pergamum (159–138 BC), this majestic two-storey stoa has 45 Doric columns on the ground floor and Ionic columns on the upper gallery. The stoa was destroyed in 267 AD by the Heruli (a Germanic tribe), but reconstructed between 1953 and 1956 by the American School of Archaeology, and, originally, the facade was painted red and blue.

Agora Museum

The excellent Agora Museum is housed inside the Stoa of Attalos. It is a great place to start, as it gives context to the site and has a model of the Agora to help get an overview. The museum displays an excellent collection of finds from the site, with a special emphasis on early Athenian democracy. Artefacts range from early voting ballots and an ancient clock to coins and terracotta figurines. Some of the oldest finds date from 4000 BC.

Ancient Statues

Around the stoa's balconies you will find magnificent marble and bronze statues of the Greek gods. The sculptures date from 5th century BC to the 3rd century AD. Look for the two Nike statues, one in bronze, with inlaid eyes, as well as a winged interpretation in marble.

GARRY BLACK/GETTY IMAGES ©

☑ Top Tips

▶ There are a number of entrances, but the most convenient is the northern entrance on Adrianou, easily accessible from the metro and Monastiraki's flea market.

▶ Save time for the museum – it is packed with superb ancient artefacts.

▶ Have a photo op at the Temple of Hephaestus – it's one of the best-preserved temples in Greece and you can get quite close to it.

▶ Hours change frequently. Call ahead to check: sometimes the Agora is open til 8pm.

✕ Take a Break

The site of the Agora today is a lush, refreshing change from congested city streets. To sit a spell, exit the northern entrance onto Adrianou, where you can enjoy a coffee or a meal at Kuzina (p51) or Dioskouri (p52).

Temple of Hephaestus

The best-preserved Doric temple in Greece, this gem on the western edge of the Agora was dedicated to Hephaestus, god of the forge, and was surrounded by foundries and metalwork shops. Built in 449 BC by Iktinos, one of the architects of the Parthenon, it has 34 columns and a frieze on the eastern side depicting nine of the Twelve Labours of Heracles. In AD 1300 it was converted into the Church of Agios Georgios.

Stoa Foundations

To the northeast of the Temple of Hephaestus lie the foundations of the **Stoa of Zeus Eleutherios**, one of the places where Socrates expounded his philosophy. Further north are the foundations of the **Stoa of Basileios** and the **Stoa Poikile**. The Stoa Poikile means Painted Stoa; it was so-called because of its murals, which were rendered by the leading artists of the day and depicted mythological and historical battles.

Council House & Tholos

Though the Turks built a residential quarter throughout the Agora, it was demolished by archaeologists after Independence and later excavated to what you see today. To the southeast of the Temple of Hephaestus they found the New Bouleuterion (Council House), where the Senate (originally created by Solon) met, while the heads of government met to the south at the circular Tholos.

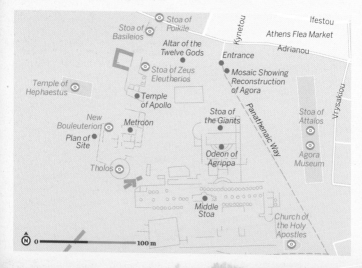

Understand
Panathenaic Procession

The biggest event in ancient Athens was the Panathenaic Procession, the climax of the Panathenaia Festival held to venerate the goddess Athena. The **Lesser Panathenaic Festival** took place annually on Athena's birthday, while the **Great Panathenaic Festival** was held on every fourth anniversary of her birth.

The Great Panathenaic Festival began with dancing, followed by athletic, dramatic and musical contests. On the final day, the Panathenaic Procession began at Keramikos, where many of the animals sacrificed to Athena were eaten at the Pompeion. The procession was led by men carrying sacrificial animals, followed by maidens carrying *rhytons* (horn-shaped drinking vessels) and musicians playing a fanfare for the girls of noble birth who held aloft the sacred *peplos* (a glorious saffron-coloured shawl). The **Panathenaic Way**, which cuts across the Ancient Agora and the middle of the Acropolis, was the route taken by the procession. The *peplos* was ultimately placed on the statue of Athena Polias in the Erechtheion in the festival's grand finale.

Church of the Holy Apostles

This charming little Byzantine church, near the southern entrance, was built in the early 10th century to commemorate St Paul's teaching in the Agora. During the period of Ottoman rule it underwent many changes, but between 1954 and 1957 it was stripped of its 19th-century additions and restored to its original form. It contains several fine Byzantine frescoes, which were transferred from a demolished church.

Local Life
Exploring Monastiraki

Emerging at Monastiraki station you are confronted with all of Athens' chaos and charm, grit and ancient splendour – the Acropolis looming above, souvlaki aromas wafting from Mitropoleos and the bustling flea market filling tiny pedestrian-only lanes. Wander the warren of shops and ateliers, dine at popular cafes and restaurants or simply people-watch in Plateia Monastirakiou (Monastiraki Sq).

❶ Plateia Avyssinias
Start your day with coffee at **Loukoumi** (Plateia Avyssinias 3, Monastiraki; Ⓜ Monastiraki), one flight above quaint Plateia Avyssinias. This cafe's unique tables and chairs evoke the furniture market below. From there, explore the antique vendors around the *plateia*.

❷ Monastiraki Flea Market
Join the hordes of locals combing Athens' flea market. This eclectic sprawl

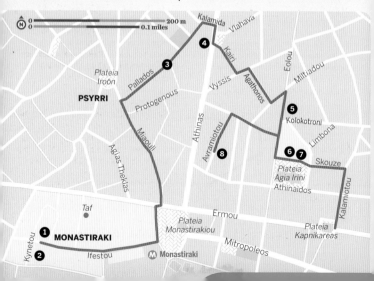

is *the* place to stumble on anything from military boots, old books and antiques to furniture and collectables. It's in its element on Sundays, when vendors line up along Adrianou, cafes reach bursting and the area rings with a festive atmosphere.

❸ Pallados Street

Wander the length of this eclectic shopping street, from chichi **Tonic Essentials** (☏210 331 7371; Pallados 24-26, Psyrri; Ⓜ Monastiraki) with its sweet array of perfumes and soaps, to **AD Gallery** (☏210 322 8785; www.adgallery.gr; Pallados 3, Psyrri; ☺noon-9pm Tue-Fri, to 4pm Sat, closed Aug; Ⓜ Monastiraki), home to cutting-edge contemporary Greek artists. At its end, vendors hawk baskets and an industrial rope store offers cords in every material and colour.

❹ Equestrian Crafts

Mompso (☏210 323 0670; www.mompso. com; Athinas 33, Psyrri; Ⓜ Monastiraki) is not to be missed. Find all manner of equestrian supplies and traditional accessories for donkeys (beaded head-dresses), shepherds (bronze bells) and country folk (walking sticks) – they make unique souvenirs and gifts.

❺ Mama Roux for Lunch

Mama Roux (☏213 004 8382; Eoulou 48-50, Monastiraki; mains €5-10; ☺9am-midnight Tue-Sat, to 5pm Mon, noon-5pm Sun; 🛜; Ⓜ Monastiraki), downtown's hottest cheap-eats restaurant, fills up with locals digging into a fresh, delicious mix of food: from real burritos and Cajun specials to

whopping American-style burgers. Reserve ahead for this popular hang-out with Santorini's Yellow Donkey beer on tap and Sunday jazz brunches.

❻ Top Souvlaki

If you're more in the mood for Greek, head to Plateia Agia Irini, to **Kostas** (☏210 323 2971; Plateia Agia Irini 2, Monastiraki; souvlaki €2; ☺9am-5pm; Ⓜ Monastiraki). At this tiny hole-in-the-wall young Kosta continues his grandfather's tradition, churning out tasty pork souvlaki with his signature spicy tomato sauce.

❼ Afternoon Pick-Me-Up

Wander the textile shops on Kalamioutou, then circle back to Plateaia Agia Irini and **Tailor Made** (☏213 004 9645; www.tailormade.gr; Plateia Agia Irini 2, Monastiraki; Ⓜ Monastiraki), the super-popular micro-roastery with fab coffees, hand-pressed teas, homemade desserts and sandwiches. Cheerful Athenians spill out onto tables alongside the flower market. At night it's a happening cocktail and wine bar.

❽ Hit the Clubs

Multi-use spaces morph from gallery to cafe to bar. **Taf's** (The Art Foundation; ☏210 323 8757; www.theartfoundation.gr; Normanou 5, Monastiraki; ☺1pm-midnight; Ⓜ Monastiraki) central courtyard cafe-bar fills with a diverse young crowd. Its art, music and theatre spaces are often free. **Six DOGS** (☏210 321 0510; www.sixdogs.gr; Avramiotou 6, Monastiraki; Ⓜ Monastiraki) has a garden courtyard for quiet chats, while the bar jams at night...theatre and art too.

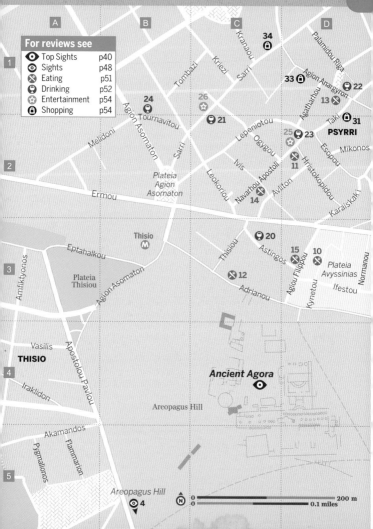

A   B   C   D

For reviews see

⊙ Top Sights	p40
⊙ Sights	p48
⊗ Eating	p51
⊖ Drinking	p52
★ Entertainment	p54
🔒 Shopping	p54

Kranaou

34 🔒

Palamidiou Riga

Tombazi

Kriezi

Sarri

Agion Anargyron

33 🔒

22

13 ⊗

Agatharhou

Taki 🔒 31

PSYRRI

24 ⊖

Tournavitou

Agion Asomaton

26 ★

21 ⊖

Lepeniotou

25 ★ ⊗ 23

Ogygou

11 ⊗

Esopou

Mikonos

Melidoni

Sarri

Ivis

Leokoriou

Navarhou Apostoli

Hristokopidou

Avliton

Karaiskaki

Plateia Agion Asomaton

Ermou

14 ⊗

Thisio Ⓜ

Thisiou

20 ⊖

Astingos

15 ⊗

10 ⊗

Normanou

Plateia Avyssinias

Agiou Filipou

Kynetou

Ifestou

Eptahalkou

Agion Asomaton

12 ⊗

Adrianou

Amfiktyonos

Plateia Thisiou

Vasilis

THISIO

Apostolou Pavlou

Iraklidon

Ancient Agora ⊙

Areopagus Hill

Akamandos

Flammarion

Pygmalionos

Areopagus Hill

4 ⊙

Ⓝ

0 —————— 200 m
0 —————— 0.1 miles

E

◎ A.antonopoulou.art **9**

Aristofanous

Estylou

Agiou Dimitriou

✕ **17**

Plateia Iroon

Pallados

Protogenous

Agias Theklas

Miaouli

Themidos

Kevitos

🔒 **29**

🔒 **32**

F

Polyklitou

Kodrika

Vyssis

🛈

Voreou

Athinas

Avramiotou

Karori

Aglas Irinis

Ermou

Plateia Monastirakiou

Plateia Dimopratiriou

16 ✕

7 ◎ **27** 🔒

G

Hrysospiliotissis

Agathonos

Eolou

Nikiou

Flower Market

Limbona

Skouze

Plateia Agia Irini

18
🛈

Athinaidos

Church of **5**
Kapnikarea ◎

H

Praxitelous

Ag.Markou

Leoharous

Kolokotroni

Klitiou

Romvis

Perikleous

Plateia Kapnikareas

Plateia Kapnikareas

1

2

3

Nisiou

19
🛈

Monastiraki Ⓜ

MONASTIRAKI

Adrianou

🔒
30

6 ◎

Hadrian's Library

Vrysakiou

Kladou

Peikilis

Taxiarhon

Dioskouron

Mitroou

Areos

Museum of Traditional Greek Ceramics

🔒 **28**

Pandrosou

Kalogrioni

Plateia Arhaia Agoras

Eolou

Pelopida

Fethiye Djami Mosque

Panos

Dexippou

Epaminonda

Roman ◎ **1**
Agora

2 ◎

Tower of the Winds

Markou Aureliou

Thrasyvoulou

Kaparikareas

Mnisikleous

Adrianou

Diogenous

Vlahou Ang.

Kalamiotou

Mitropoleos

Plateia Mitropoleos

3 ◎
Athens Cathedral & Little Metropolis

PLAKA

Agias Filotheis

8 ◎
Turkish Baths

Kyrristou

Lyssiou

Flessa

4

5

Sights

Roman Agora   ANCIENT SITE

1 ◉ Map p46, F5

Enter the Romans' civic centre
through the well-preserved **Gate of
Athena Archegetis**, which is flanked
by four Doric columns. It was erected
sometime during the 1st century AD
and financed by Julius Caesar. At this
partly excavated site, you can see the
foundations of several structures,
including a 1st-century, 68-seat public
latrine to the right of the entry, and a
propylon (entrance) at the south-
eastern corner. The **Fethiye Djami
mosque** on the northern side of the
Agora is one of the city's few surviving
reminders of Ottoman times. (✆210
324 5220; cnr Pelopida & Eolou, Monastiraki;
adult/child €2/1, with Acropolis pass free;
⊘8.30am-3pm; M Monastiraki)

Tower of
the Winds   ANCIENT MONUMENT

2 ◉ Map p46, F5

The well-preserved Tower of the
Winds was built in the 1st century BC
by Syrian astronomer Andronicus.
The octagonal marble construction
functioned as an ingenious sundial, weather vane, water clock and
compass. Each side represents a point
of the compass, and has a relief of a
figure depicting the wind associated
with that point. Beneath each relief
are the faint markings of sundials.
The weather vane, which disappeared
long ago, was a bronze Triton that
revolved on top of the tower. (Roman
Agora)

Athens Cathedral &
Little Metropolis   CHURCHES

3 ◉ Map p46, H4

The ornate 1862 Athens Cathedral
is the seat of the archbishop of the
Greek Orthodox Church of Athens.
Far more significant historically and
architecturally is the small 12th-
century church next to it. Known as
Little Metropolis, its official double-
barrelled name is Church of Panagia
Gorgeopikoos (Virgin Swift to Hear)
and Agios Eleftherios. This marble
church was built on the ruins of an
ancient temple and incorporates
reliefs and pieces of ancient and early-
Christian monuments. (✆210 322 1308;
Plateia Mitropoleos, Monastiraki; ⊘7am-7pm,
Sun Mass 6.30am; M Monastiraki)

Areopagus Hill   LANDMARK, PARK

4 ◉ Map p46, B5

This rocky outcrop has superb views
over the Ancient Agora. According to
mythology, it was here that Ares was
tried by the council of the gods for the
murder of Halirrhothios, son of Poseidon. The hill became the place where
murder, treason and corruption trials
were heard. In AD 51 St Paul delivered
his famous 'Sermon to an Unknown
God' here and gained his first Athenian convert, Dionysos. (admission free;
M Monastiraki)

Understand

Roman Rule

- -

The First Incursions

During the 4th century BC, while Alexander the Great of Macedon was ruling the Greek city-states and forging his vast empire through Persia and into the east, the Romans were expanding their empire to the west, and began making in-roads into Greece. After Alexander's death in 323 BC, Macedonia lost control of the southern Greek city-states, which banded together into the Aetolian League, centred on Delphi, and the Achaean League, based in the Peloponnese. Athens and Sparta joined neither.

Roman Victories

After several inconclusive clashes, the Romans finally defeated Macedon in 168 BC at the Battle of Pydna. The Achaean League was defeated in 146 BC and the Roman consul Mummius made an example of the rebellious Corinthians by destroying their city.

In 86 BC Athens joined an ill-fated rebellion against the Romans in Asia Minor staged by the king of the Black Sea region, Mithridates VI. In retribution, the fierce Roman statesman Sulla invaded Athens, destroyed the city walls and carted off many of its finest statues to Rome. At this point, Greece became the Graeco-Roman province of Achaea. Although officially under the auspices of Rome, several major Greek cities were given the freedom to self-govern to some extent.

The Pax Romana

Because the Romans revered Greek culture, Athens retained its status as a centre of learning. The city received a pardon for its rebellion from Julius Caesar and, for the next 300 years, it experienced an unprecedented period of peace – the Pax Romana. During this time it became the seat of learning for the Romans as well, attracting the sons of wealthy Romans. During the Pax Romana, a succession of Roman emperors, namely Augustus, Nero and particularly Hadrian, graced Athens with many grand buildings, including the Roman Agora, Hadrian's library (p50) and territorial **arch** (cnr Leoforos Vasilissis Olgas & Leoforos Vasilissis Amalias; M Syntagma).

The Pax Romana lasted until the middle of the 3rd century AD, and was followed by the decline of the Roman Empire and the rise of the Byzantine Empire, centred around Constantinople (modern-day Istanbul).

(IZZET KERIBAR/GETTY IMAGES ©)

Church of Kapnikarea

Church of Kapnikarea   CHURCH

5 ◉ Map p46, G3

This small 11th-century Byzantine church stands smack in the middle of the Ermou shopping strip. It was saved from the bulldozers and restored by Athens University. The dome of this cruciform-style church is supported by four large Roman columns. (Ermou, Monastiraki; ⏰8am-2pm Tue, Thu & Fri; Ⓜ Monastiraki)

Hadrian's Library   RUINS

6 ◉ Map p46, E4

Once the most luxurious public building in the city, Hadrian's library was erected around AD 132. It had an internal courtyard and pool bordered by 100 columns. The building was

destroyed in AD 267 during the Herulian invasion. The remains of Megali Panagia, believed to be the oldest Christian church in Athens, can be seen in the garden, including parts of the mosaic floor. During the Ottoman period it was a bazaar. (Areos, Monastiraki; admission €2; Ⓜ Monastiraki)

Museum of Traditional Greek Ceramics   MUSEUM

7 ◉ Map p46, F3

The Mosque of Tzistarakis (built in 1759) is one of few surviving examples of a *tzami* (mosque) in Athens. It houses this annexe of the Museum of Greek Folk Art and features pottery and hand-painted ceramics from the early 20th century. (📞210 324 2066; Areos 1, Monastiraki; adult/child €2/free; Ⓜ Monastiraki)

Turkish Baths   ANCIENT SITE

8 ◉ Map p46, G5

The only surviving public bathhouse in Athens is one of the few remnants of the Ottoman period. The refurbished 17th-century bathhouse of Abit Efendi gives some insight into the rituals of the era, when bathhouses were an important meeting point. (📞210 324 4340; Kyristou 8, Monastiraki; admission €2; ⏰9am-2.30pm Tue-Sun; Ⓜ Monastiraki)

A.antonopoulou.art   GALLERY

9 ◉ Map p46, E1

One of the original galleries to open in Psyrri's warehouses, this impressive art space hosts a range of exhibitions of contemporary and international art, including installations, video art and photography by emerging Greek artists. (📞 210 321 4994; www.aaart.gr; Aristofanous 20, 4th fl, Psyrri; Ⓜ Monastiraki)

Eating

Café Avyssinia TRADITIONAL GREEK €€

10 Map p46, D3

Hidden away on colourful Plateia Avyssinias, this bohemian *mezedhopoleio* gets top marks for atmosphere, food and friendly service. It specialises in regional Greek cuisine, from warm fava to eggplants baked with tomato and cheese, and has a great selection of ouzo, *raki* (Cretan firewater) and *tsipouro*. Weekends see acoustic live music. Snag fantastic Acropolis views from the seats upstairs. (📞 210 321 7047; www.avissinia.gr; Kynetou 7, Monastiraki; mains €10-16; ⏱ 11am-1am Tue-Sat, to 7pm Sun; Ⓜ Monastiraki)

Hytra FINE DINING €€€

11 Map p46, D2

This tiny chute of a restaurant is decked out in oil paintings of bikes and motorcycles... Oh, yes, and has one Michelin star. One of Athens' haute-cuisine hideouts, Hytra serves up exquisitely presented Greek food with a modern twist. In summer it moves to the Westin Athens, Astir Palace Beach Resort in coastal Vouliagmeni. (📞 210 331 6767; www.hytra.

gr; Navarhou Apostoli 7, Psyrri; mains €28-30; ⏱ dinner Tue-Sun; Ⓜ Thisio)

Kuzina MODERN GREEK €€

12 Map p46, C3

Light streams through the plate-glass windows here, warming the crowded tables in winter. Or eat outside on pedestrianised people-watching Adrianou in summer. The modern mood and music set the tone for inventive Greek fusion, like Cretan pappardelle or chicken with figs and sesame. (📞 210 324 0133; www.kuzina.gr; Adrianou 9, Monastiraki; mains €12-25; Ⓜ Thisio)

Nikitas TAVERNA €

13 Map p46, D1

Locals swear by this old taverna that has been serving reasonably priced, refreshingly simple and tasty traditional food since well before Psyrri became trendy. (📞 210 325 2591; Agion Anargyron 19, Psyrri; mains €6; ⏱ noon-6pm; Ⓜ Monastiraki)

Local Life
Mezedhes & Ouzo

Join young Athenians at **Kalipateira** (📞 210 321 4152; Astingos 8, Monastirkai; Ⓜ Monastiraki) as they gather for long sessions over carafes of ouzo, snacking on one of the *pikilies* (mixed mezedhes). Thursday to Sunday acoustic *rembetika* (Greek blues) and Cretan live music rocks out this neoclassic building overlooking an archaeological dig.

Ivis

MEZEDHES €€

14 Map p46, C2

This cosy corner spot with bright, arty decor, has a small but delicious range of simple, freshly cooked mezedhes. Ask for the daily specials as there's only a rough Greek hand-written menu. A good ouzo selection lights things up. (210 323 2554; Navarhou Apostoli 19, Psyrri; mezedhes €4-10; Thisio)

Ouzou Melathron

TAVERNA €

15 Map p46, D3

This successful Thessaloniki restaurant is a bit gimmicky, with goofy, oversized menus, but the food does not disappoint. Friendly service and a range of creative mezedhes make it one of the better offerings in the area. (210 324 0716; Agiou Filipou 10, cnr Astingos, Monastiraki; mezedhes €5-7; Monastiraki)

 Local Life

Hot Grill

Telis (210 324 2775; Evripidou 86, Psyrri; pork chops €7; 8am-2am Mon-Sat; Thisio) has been slaving over the flame grill at this fluoro-lit, bare-walled, paper-tablecloth *psistaria*, cooking his famous pork chops, since 1978. There's nothing else on the menu – just meat, chips and Greek salad, washed down with rough house wine or beer.

Thanasis

SOUVLAKI €

16 Map p46, F3

In the heart of Athens' souvlaki hub at the end of Mitropoleos, Thanasis is known for its kebabs on pitta with grilled tomato and onions. Live music, wafting grill aromas and constant crowds give the area an almost permanently festive air. (210 324 4705; Mitropoleos 69, Monastiraki; gyros €2.50; 8.30am-2.30am; Monastiraki)

Taverna Tou Psyrri

TAVERNA €

17 Map p46, E1

This age-old cheerful taverna just off Plateia Iroön turns out decent, no-frills, traditional food, either street-side or in an interior garden. (210 321 4923; Eshylou 12, Psyrri; mains €6-8; closed 2wks Aug; Monastiraki)

Drinking

Magaze

CAFE, BAR

18 Map p46, G2

With tables on the pedestrian strip at Plateia Agia Irinis looking up to the Acropolis, this gay-friendly place is popular day and night. If you're lost you can check out the large-scale Athens map on the wall. (210 324 3740; Eolou 33, Monastiraki; Monastiraki)

Dioskouri

CAFE, MODERN GREEK

19 Map p46, E3

A landmark cafe sitting virtually over the railway line, the tables under a

GEORGE TSAFOS/GETTY IMAGES ©

Dining at Ouzou Melathron

huge plane tree give it a traditional village feel. It's popular with students for mezedhes and ouzo. (Adrianou 37, Monastiraki; **M** Monastiraki)

James Joyce
PUB

20 Map p46, C3

With freeflowing Guinness and tasty burgers and pub food, this rather incongruous Irish pub is a magnet for the expat crowd. (☎ 210 323 5055; Astingos 12, Monastiraki; mains €9-14; **M** Monastiraki)

Alekos' Island
GAY BAR

21 Map p46, C2

One of Athens' oldest and friendliest gay bars has been relocated from Kolonaki to this stylish venue. Alekos,

the artist-owner, is behind the bar (some of his work adorns the walls), while partner Jean Pierre plays DJ. Attracts a mixed crowd. (☎ 210 723 9163; Sarri 41, Psyrri; **M** Thisio)

Second Skin
BAR

22 Map p46, D1

Athens' premier goth-industrial venue holds torture garden parties and the like. (www.secondskinclub.gr; Plateia Agion Anargyron 5, Psyrri; **M** Thisio)

Thirio
BAR

23 Map p46, D2

A Psyrri veteran, the delightful two-level warren of small nooks and lounges offers eclectic music and unique ambience. (Lepeniotou 1, Psyrri; **M** Thisio)

Local Life

Faust

One of the city's hottest new bars, **Faust** (210 323 4095; www.faust.gr; Kalamiotou 11 & Athinaidos 12; ⊘closed Jun-Aug; Monastiraki), just a tiny hole in the wall, also hosts live music, cabarets, and art shows. The decor is louche bordello meets neoclassical Greek...and the crowds are lively.

El Pecado
CLUB

 24 Map p46, B1

A good bet for dancing the night away...They literally ring a church bell to fire up the 30-something crowd. In summer it moves beachside to Glyfada. (210 324 4049; www.elpecado.gr; Tournavitou 11, Psyrri; ⊘closed Jun-Sep; Thisio)

Entertainment

Paliogramofono
MUSIC TAVERNA

25 Map p46, D2

People come here for the chance to hear live Greek music, not so much for the food. Call ahead to make sure something will be on. (210 323 1409; Navarhou Apostoli 8, Psyrri; Thisio)

Cine Psyrri
CINEMA

26 Map p46, C1

This charming outdoor cinema on a rooftop garden terrace is a great place to get some relief from the heat and

crowds. (210 324 7234; Sarri 40-44, Psyrri; Thisio)

Shopping

Martinos
ANTIQUES

 27 Map p46, F3

This Monastiraki landmark opened in 1890 and has an excellent selection of Greek and European antiques and collectables, including painted dowry chests, icons, coins and much more. (210 321 2414; www.martinosart.gr; Pandrosou 50, Monastiraki; Monastiraki)

Centre of Hellenic Tradition
HANDICRAFTS

 28 Map p46, F3

Upstairs in this arcade are great examples of traditional ceramics, sculptures, woodcarvings, paintings and folk art from prominent Greek artists. The quaint cafe-*ouzerie* has Acropolis views. (210 321 3023; Pandrosou 36, Monastiraki; Monastiraki)

 Top Tip

Cafe Denizens

Monastiraki's **Adrianou** street and Psyrri's **Agiou Anargyrou** are loaded with cafes that turn into bars at night. And though coffee in Athens is some of the most expensive in Europe (think €3 to €5), you'll get the table for as long as you like. Tops for people-watching!

Melissinos Art
CLOTHING, ACCESSORIES

29 🔒 Map p46, E3

Athens' famous sandal-maker and poet, septuagenarian Stavros Melissinos, has pretty much handed the reins to artist son Pantelis, who continues making classic leather sandals modelled on ancient styles, and adds his own touch to more than 32 designs. His daughter Olgianna Melissinos makes beautiful handbags and takes custom orders. (☏ 210 321 9247; www.melissinos-art.com; Agias Theklas 2, Psyrri; Ⓜ Monastiraki)

Spiliopoulos
SHOES, CLOTHING

30 🔒 Map p46, E4

More spacious than the original Ermou store, this is the place to try to nab bargain designer and imported shoes, handbags, leather jackets and clothes. (☏ 210 321 9096; Adrianou 50, Monastiraki; Ⓜ Monastiraki)

Kartousa
JEWELLERY, HOMEWARES

31 🔒 Map p46, D2

Ecelctic handmade jewellery and housewares brighten this tiny storefront. (☏ 210 324 7525; Taki 9, Psyrri; Ⓜ Monastiraki)

Carnaby St
CLOTHING

32 🔒 Map p46, E3

Designer streetwear, including London labels, as well as a range of funky T-shirts from Greek brand Fingerprint in this new cluster of trendy clothing stores. (☏ 210 331 5333; Ermou 99 , cnr Normanou, Monastiraki; Ⓜ Monastiraki)

Sabater Hermanos
SOAP

33 🔒 Map p46, D1

This itsy-bitsy, bright and cheery shop is packed with colourful all-natural soaps and bath crystals. (☏ 210 331 6824; Agion Anargyron 31, Psyrri; Ⓜ Thisio)

Mofu
INTERIOR DESIGN

34 🔒 Map p46, C1

Retro fans will adore the eclectic range of largely '50s, '60s and '70s furniture, lamps and odd designer collectables at this friendly store. Shipping can be arranged if you just have to have that piece. (☏ 210 331 9220; Sarri 28, Psyrri; Ⓜ Thisio)

Local Life
Wandering Central Market

Getting There

M **Metro** Three stations serve the market equally well: Monastiraki (blue and green lines), Omonia (red and green lines), Panepistimio (red line).

The streets around the colourful and bustling Athens Central Market (also referred to as the Varvakios Agora) are a sensory delight. Jam-packed with people shopping at the market – the highlight of the district – and at nearby spice and provisions shops, it also harbours some of *the* most classic local eating experiences, the city's best *rembetika* (Greek blues) joint, and cutting-edge art galleries.

① Athens Central Market

The hectic, colourful **Athens Central Market** (Varvakios Agora; Athinas , btwn Sofokleous & Evripidou; ⊙7am-3pm Mon-Sat) is an explosion for the senses and a must for gastronomes, with an amazing range of olives, spices, cheeses and deli treats. Filling the historic building on the eastern side, the **meat and fish market**, with its hanging carcasses illuminated by swinging light bulbs, is a surreal highlight. The **fruit and vegetable market** is across the road.

② Spice Shops & More

Along the streets around the market, burlap bags overflow with chilis, dried rosebuds, candied ginger, and many more things than one can imagine. Wander the shops enjoying the aromas emanating from within. **Miran** (☎210 321 7187; www.miran.gr; Evripidou 45) is the local favourite for prepared meats from sausage to prosciutto.

③ Greek Regional Specialties

If you'd like a more structured shopping experience, head straight to **To Pantopoleion** (☎210 323 4612; Sofokleous 1, Omonia), an expansive store selling traditional food products from all over Greece. Find everything from Santorini capers to Cretan rusks, jars of goodies, and Greek wines and spirits.

④ Quirky Taverna

There's no signage at **Diporto Agoras** (☎210 321 1463; cnr Theatrou & Sokratous; plates €5-6; ⊙8am-6pm Mon-Sat, closed 1-20 Aug), one of the dining gems of Athens.

Double doors lead to a rustic cellar, where there's also no menu. The speciality is *revythia* (chickpeas), followed by grilled fish and washed down with wine from giant barrels. Often-erratic service is part of the appeal.

⑤ Hot Contemporary Art

After lunch, hit two of Athens' most innovative modern art galleries, which promote young, emerging local and visiting artists: **Qbox Gallery** (☎211 119 9991; www.qbox.gr; Armodiou 10; ⊙noon-6pm Tue-Fri, to 4pm Sat) and **Andreas Melas & Helena Papadopoulos Gallery** (☎210 325 1881; http://melaspapadopoulos. com; Epikourou 26, cnr Korinis, Psyrri; ⊙noon-6pm Tue-Fri, to 4pm Sat).

⑥ Late-Night Dinner

The meat market might sound like a strange place to go for a meal, but the tavernas, such as **Papandreou** (☎213 008 2242; Aristogitonos 1; mains €7-8; ⊙24hr), are an Athenian institution, turning out huge quantities of tasty, traditional fare for everyone from hungry market workers to late-night partiers.

⑦ Rembetika

The legendary *rembetika* club **Stoa Athanaton** (☎210 321 4362; Sofokleous 19; ⊙3-6pm & midnight-6am Mon-Sat, closed Jun-Sep) occupies a hall above the central meat market. It remains *the* place to hear classic *rembetika* and *laïka* (urban popular music) from a respected band of musicians. It often starts from mid-afternoon and access is by a lift in the arcade.

Explore

Greek Parliament, Syntagma & Plaka

Syntagma is the heart of modern Athens, with Plateia Syntagmatos (Syntagma Sq) its historic meeting point, political centre and transport hub. The National Gardens offer respite from the hustle, or it's a short walk to Plaka, which has an undeniable charm. Its paved, narrow streets pass by ancient sites, restored and crumbling neoclassical mansions, small museums, Byzantine churches and ambient tavernas.

The Sights in a Day

☀ Start your day by exploring Athens' main shopping districts in Plaka and Syntagma. From creative jewellery like that at **Apriati** (p72), to handicrafts at **Aidini** (p71) or backgammon sets at **Ekavi** (p72), there's so much to see your head will be spinning. Break for lunch at a simple taverna like **Paradosiako** (p68), or eat organic at **Pure Bliss** (p69).

☼ Visit the vast array of museums of Greek culture **Kanellopoulos Museum** (p64), **Greek Folk Art Museum** (p66) and art, the **National Museum of Contemporary Art** (p64), or watch the **Changing of the Guard** (p64) and then hide from the heat in the verdant **National Gardens** (p64).

☾ Dine at **Tzitzikas & Mermingas** (p67), then go bar hopping around Syntagma at places such as **Seven Jokers** (p69), **Galaxy Bar** (p70), **Bartessera** (p69) and **Barley Cargo** (p70). Or for a more sedate evening, catch a flick at **Cine Paris** (p71), Plaka's outdoor cinema.

For a local's day in Plaka, see p60.

Q Local Life

Shopping Around Plaka (p60)

♥ Best of Athens

Museums

Kanellopoulos Museum (p64)

Greek Folk Art Museum (p66)

Jewish Museum (p66)

Bars

Seven Jokers (p69)

Brettos (p70)

Barley Cargo (p70)

Galaxy Bar (p70)

Baba Au Rum (p69)

Gin Joint (p61)

Bartessera (p69)

Getting There

Ⓜ **Metro** The Syntagma station (blue and red lines) sits at the heart of the city. You'll emerge right at Plateia Syntagmatos, which is a short walk to Plaka.

Ⓜ **Metro** Plaka is also easily reached from the Monastiraki station (blue and green lines) to the north, and the Akropoli station (red line) to the southwest.

Local Life
Shopping Around Plaka

Plaka's lower reaches are jammed with small museums, slews of tavernas, and kitsch souvenir stores, especially on main streets like Kydathineon and Adrianou. Move away from the tourist strip for a glimpse of old Athens – virtually car-free – in narrow lanes winding up the northeastern side of the Acropolis hill, and in the maze of the Anafiotika quarter. A jaunt north to the Syntagma area will bring you to Athens' hippest bar precinct.

❶ Breakfast Homage to Melina
Low-key **Melina** (Lysiou 22, Plaka; Ⓜ Akropoli, Monastiraki) is an ode to the late, great Mercouri. Decorated with memorabilia and photographs celebrating Greece's legendary actress and politician, it offers charm and intimacy out of the hectic centre.

❷ Shopping Adrianou
Plaka is loaded with so-so vendors – instead, head to its best shops, the

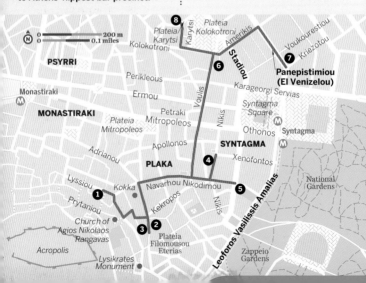

ones Athenians frequent. **Ioanna Kourbela** (210 322 4591; www.ioannak ourbela.com; Adrianou 109 & Hatzimihali 12, Plaka; MSytnatgma) designs classic, cool women's clothes: elegantly draped cottons and silks in natural, warm tones.

3 Accessorise It!

Ikonomou (210 935 5493; www.kreitto.gr; Adrianou 130, Plaka; MSyntagma) creates unique contemporary designs that combine silver with materials like coral, onyx and turquoise. At **Kokka** (210 322 4460; Adrianou 114, Plaka; MSyntagma) kit yourself out for the seaside with locally made leather sandals: strappy for evening, funky for day.

4 Snacks & Wine

Avocado (210 323 7878; www. avocadoathens.com; Nikis 30, Plaka; mains €6.50-9.50; 11am-10pm Mon-Sat, to 7pm Sun; ; MSyntagma) dishes up vegan, gluten-free, and organic treats – a rarity in Greece. Enjoy everything from sandwiches to coconut curry on the tiny front patio. Juices and smoothies are made on the spot, or splash out on a bottle at **Wine Story** (210 323 9997; www.winestory.gr; Nikis 21, Plaka; 9am-9.30pm Mon-Sat, 10am-2pm & 5-9pm Sun; MSyntagma), across the street.

5 Byzantine Churches

Break from shopping and visit **Sotira Lykodimou**, built in 1031. It is the largest medieval structure (and only octagonal Byzantine church) in Athens, and has served as the Russian Orthodox Church since 1847. The 11th-

century **Agios Nikolaos Rangavas** was part of the palace of the Rangava family, which included Michael I, emperor of Byzantium.

6 Chocolate Indulgence

For a sweet pick-me-up head to **Aristokratikon** (210 322 0546; www. aristokratikon.com; Voulis 7, Syntagma; MSyntagma), where chocoholics will be thrilled by the dazzling array of handmade chocolates at this tiny store that's been around since 1928. Karageorgi Servias is also loaded with sweet and dried nut shops.

7 Mastiha Shop

While you're in the neighbourhood, swing over to **Mastiha Shop** (210 363 2750; www.mastihashop.com; Panepistimiou 6, Syntagma; 9am-9pm; MSyntagma), purveyor of all things mastic: the medicinal resin from rare mastic trees produced only on the island of Chios. The liqueur is divine when served chilled, but there's also skin products, essential oils and foodstuffs.

8 Clubbing in Syntagma

After you've rested up and grabbed some nourishment for the night, head to the area around Plateia Karytsi and Kolokotroni for central Athens' best bar scene. One such, they call **Gin Joint** (Lada 1, Syntagma; MSyntagma) for a reason: sample 60 gins or other fancy cocktails, some with historical notes on their origin.

A B C D

1

Vyssis
Miltiadou
Praxitelous
9 City of Athens Museum
Plateia Karytsi

15

Athinas
Avramiotou
Karori
Nikiou
Limbona
23
Pavlou
Havrou
Karytsi
Gaz Anthimou

Skouze
Klitiou
20
Romvis
25
21
Kolokotroni

2

Athinaidos
16
17
Thiseos
Leka

MONASTIRAKI

Ermou
Perikleous
Diomias
Axarlian

Plateia Kapnikareas
Evangelistrias
Fokionos

Monastiraki Pandrosou
Mitropoleos
Petraki
38

3

Dexippou
Eolou
Plateia Mitropoleos
Ipatias
Patrodu
Pendelis

Adrianou
Benizelou Paleologou
Apollonos
41

Pelopida
Museum of Greek Popular Instruments
10
Mnisikleous
Aglas Filotheis
Thoukididou
Ipitou
PLAKA
Voulis

14
12

4

Thrasyvoulou
27
31
Kyrristou
Navarhou Nikodimou
36
Kodrou

Lyssiou
30
Flessa
Adrianou
Iperidou

Kanellopoulos Museum
5
Theorias
Erehtheos
18
Scholiou
Kekropos
Plateia Sotiros
Greek Folk Art Museum
6

Prytaniou
13

ANAFIOTIKA
29
Kydathineon

5

PLAKA
Stratonos
Tripodon
42
24
Plateia Filomousou Eterias

Acropolis
Rangava

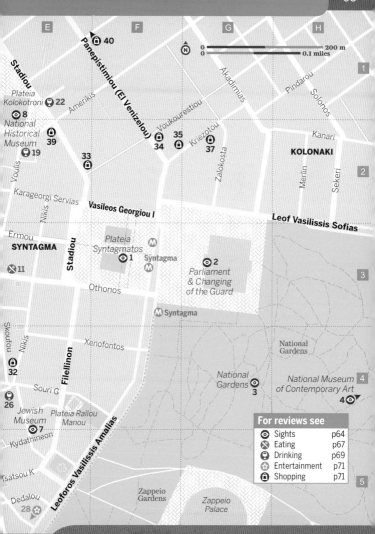

E **F** **G** **H**

Stadiou

Panepistimiou (El Venizelou)

▲ 40

Amerikis

🚇 N

0 ____ 200 m
0 ____ 0.1 miles

1

Plateia
Kolokotroni 🎯 22

🎯 8
National
Historical
Museum 🔒 39
🎯 19

Voulis

Akadimias

Pindarou

Solonos

Voukourestiou

35
🔒 34

Kriezotou

🔒 37

Kanari

KOLONAKI

2

33
🔒

Zalokosta

Merlin

Sekeri

Karageorgi Servias

Nikis

Vasileos Georgiou I

Leof Vasilissis Sofias

Ermou
SYNTAGMA

Stadiou

Plateia
Syntagmatos 🎯 1

Ⓜ
Syntagma

🎯 2
Parliament
& Changing
of the Guard

3

❌ 11

Othonos

Ⓜ Syntagma

Skoufou

Nikis

Filellinon

Xenofonts

National
Gardens

🔒 32

Souri G

National
Gardens 🎯 3

National Museum
of Contemporary Art ▲
4 🎯

4

🎯 26

Jewish
Museum
🎯 7

Plateia Rallou
Manou

Kydathineon

Leoforos Vasilissis Amalias

For reviews see

🎯 Sights   p64
❌ Eating   p67
🎯 Drinking   p69
⭐ Entertainment p71
🔒 Shopping   p71

5

Tsatsou K

Dedalou

⭐ 28

Zappeio
Gardens

Zappeio
Palace

Sights

Plateia Syntagmatos

SQUARE, MONUMENT

1 Map p62, F3

Athens's central square (Syntagma, or Constitution Sq in English) is named for the constitution granted, after uprisings, by King Otto on 3 September 1843. Today, the square serves as a major transportation hub, the location of the seat of power and also, therefore, the epicentre of demonstrations and strikes. (Syntagma Square; **M**Syntagma)

Parliament & Changing of the Guard

HISTORIC BUILDING

2 Map p62, G3

The **Tomb of the Unknown Soldier** in the forecourt of the parliament building (only the **library** is open to the public) is guarded by the city's famous statuesque *evzones*, the presidential guards whose uniform of short kilts and pom-pom shoes is based on the attire worn by the klephts (the mountain fighters of the War of Independence). The high-kicking changing of the guard occurs every hour on the hour. Sunday at 11am a whole platoon marches down Vasilissis Sofias to the tomb, accompanied by a band. (Plateia Syntagmatos, Syntagma; **M**Syntagma)

National Gardens

PARK, GARDEN

3 Map p62, G4

A delightful, shady refuge during summer, the National Gardens were formerly the royal gardens designed by Queen Amalia. There's also a large children's **playground**, a duck pond and a shady **cafe**. (entrances on Leoforos Vasilissis Sofias & Leoforos Vasilissis Amalias, Syntagma; ⏱7am-dusk; **M**Syntagma)

National Museum of Contemporary Art

ART MUSEUM

4 Map p62, H4

Housed in a temporary gallery at the Athens Conservatory, this excellently curated museum shows rotating exhibitions of Greek and international contemporary art. Exhibitions include paintings, installations, photography, video and new media, as well as experimental architecture. The museum is slated to move to the old Fix brewery on Leoforos Syngrou in October 2013. (☎210 924 2111; www.emst. gr; Leoforos Vas Georgiou B 17-19, enter from Rigilis; adult/child €3/free; ⏱11am-7pm Tue, Wed & Fri-Sun, to 10pm Thu; **M**Evangelismos)

Kanellopoulos Museum

ANTIQUITIES MUSEUM

5 Map p62, A5

This excellent museum, in a 19th-century mansion on the northern slope of the Acropolis, reopened in 2010 after renovations that doubled its size. It houses the Kanellopoulos family's extensive collection, donated to the state in 1976. The collection includes jewellery, clay and stone vases and figurines, weapons, Byzantine icons, bronzes and *objets d'art*. (☎210 321 2313; Theorias 12, cnr Panos, Plaka; ⏱9am-4pm Tue-Sun; **M**Monastiraki)

Understand

Greece's Political & Economic Situation

In December 2009 newly elected Prime Minister George Papandreou revealed to the world that Greece's debts had reached €300 billion (113% of GDP – nearly double the eurozone limit of 60%). Ratings agencies started downgrading Greek debt and the ultimate spiral of economic depression and possible default began. Greece's total debt soared, reaching 165.3% of GDP in 2011.

The Bailout

At the time of writing (July 2012) Greece had received two bailout pledges from the European Commission, the European Central Bank and the International Monetary Fund (collectively known as the 'troika' in Greece) totaling €240 billion. In return the government agreed to cut its debts to 120% of GDP by 2020, and reduce its budget deficit from 9.3% of GDP in 2011 to 3% in 2014. Each tranche of bailout funding is preceded by financial audits and negotiations. So far there has been one major restructure and more are in the works.

But the austerity measures and tax hikes demanded by the troika have added to the country's depression: GDP shrunk by about 20% during five years. Unemployment reached nearly 23% in early 2012, a record. To many, it looks like trying to squeeze blood from a stone.

The Human Costs

Throughout these events, tumultuous human, social and political repercussions have rocked Greece. These include mass protests and widespread strikes, the resignation of Papandreou in November 2011, an interim government, and two rounds of 2012 elections resulting in both the rise of the anti-bailout far left, the far right, and, ultimately, in the formation of a tenuous coalition government. The reality of lost jobs, cut wages and pensions, and disappearing social services has been exacerbated by the uncertainty that accompanies each of these political and economic manoeuvres. Meanwhile, reports of suicides caused by money worries are daily media staples (Greece historically has had the lowest rate in the EU), as are attacks on immigrants in the Athens area.

Default and exit from the eurozone remain a real possibility. In the meantime, economic trouble has spread across Europe.

GEORGE TSAFOS/GETTY IMAGES ©

Greek Folk Art Museum

Greek Folk Art Museum

CULTURAL MUSEUM

6 💿 Map p62, D5

This fine state-owned museum displays folk art from 1650 to the present, including elaborate embroidery, weaving, costumes, shadow-theatre puppets and silverwork. The 1st floor has interesting wall murals by renowned naive artist Theophilos Hatzimichail, and a temporary exhibition gallery. Its annexes are the **Greek Folk Art Museum: Man & Tools** (📞210 321 4972; Panos 22, Plaka; admission €2; ⊙8am-3pm Tue-Sun; Ⓜ Monastiraki) and the Museum of Traditional Greek Ceramics (p50). (📞210 322 9031; Kydathineon 17, Plaka; adult/child €2/free; ⊙9am-2.30pm Tue-Sun; Ⓜ Syntagma)

Jewish Museum

CULTURAL MUSEUM

7 💿 Map p62, E4

This museum traces the history of the Jewish community in Greece from the 3rd century BC, with an impressive collection of religious and historical artefacts, documents, folk art and costumes. It includes a small reconstruction of a synagogue. Nearly 90% of Greece's Jews, most from Thessaloniki, were killed during the Holocaust. (📞210 322 5582; www.jewishmuseum.gr; Nikis 39, Plaka; adult/child €6/3; ⊙9am-2.30pm Mon-Fri, 10am-2pm Sun; Ⓜ Syntagma)

National Historical Museum

HISTORY MUSEUM

8 Map p62, E1

Greece's first parliament building houses memorabilia from the War of Independence, including Byron's helmet and sword, weapons, costumes and flags, paintings, Byzantine and medieval exhibits, and photos illustrating Greece's evolution since Constantinople's fall in 1453. (✆210 323 7617; www.nhmuseum.gr; Stadiou 13, Syntagma; adult/child €3/free, Sun free; ⊗9am-2pm Tue-Sun; Ⓜ Syntagma)

City of Athens Museum

CULTURAL MUSEUM

9 Map p62, D1

Once the residence of King Otto and Queen Amalia, the museum displays some of the royal couple's personal effects and furniture – including the throne – as well as paintings by leading Greek and foreign artists, and models of 19th-century Athens. (✆210 323 1397; www.athenscitymuseum.gr; Paparigopoulou 7, Syntagma; adult/child €3/free; ⊗9am-4pm Mon & Wed-Fri, 10am-3pm Sat & Sun; Ⓜ Panepistimio)

Museum of Greek Popular Instruments

MUSIC MUSEUM

10 Map p62, B4

More than 1200 folk instruments dating from the 18th century are exhibited over three floors, with headphones for visitors to listen to the sounds of the *gaida* (Greek goatskin bagpipes) and Byzantine mandolins, among others. Musical performances are held in the lovely garden in summer. (✆210 325 4119; Diogenous 1-3, Plaka; admission free; ⊗10am-2pm Tue & Thu-Sun, noon-6pm Wed; Ⓜ Monastiraki)

Eating

Tzitzikas & Mermingas

MEZEDHES €

11 Map p62, E3

This bright and cheery modern *mezed-hopoleio* is popular for its delicious and creative mezedhes, like manouri cheese wrapped in ham and drizzled with honey. The old Greek deli theme extends from the walls of shelves lined with Greek products to the unique toilet hand basins. (✆210 324 7607; Mitropoleos 12-14, Syntagma; mezedhes €6-11; Ⓜ Syntagma)

 Local Life

Low-Key Streetside Fare

Find your way back behind the Church of Agii Theodori to **Kalnterimi** (✆210 331 0049; www.kalnterimi.gr; Plateia Agion Theodoron, cnr Skouleniou; mains €5-8; ⊗lunch & dinner; Ⓜ Panepistimio), a favourite open-air taverna offering Greek food at its most authentic. Everything is fresh-cooked and delicious: you can't go wrong. Hand-painted tables spill onto a pedestrian street and give a feeling of peace in one of the busiest parts of the city.

Paradosiako

TAVERNA €

12 | Map p62, D4

For great traditional fare, you can't beat this inconspicuous, no-frills taverna on the periphery of Plaka, with a few tables on the pavement. There's a basic menu but it's best to choose from the daily specials, which include fresh seafood like prawn *saganaki*. It fills up quickly with locals, so arrive early. (☎210 321 4121; Voulis 44a, Plaka; mains €5-11; 🛜; Ⓜ Syntagma)

Glykis

MEZEDHES €

13 | Map p62, D5

In a quiet corner of Plaka, this low-key *mezedhopoleio* with a shady courtyard is mostly frequented by students and locals. It has a tasty selection of mezedhes, including traditional dishes such as *briam* (oven-baked vegetable casserole) and cuttlefish in wine. (☎210 322 3925; Angelou Geronta 2, Plaka; mezedhes €5.50-6; ⏱10.30am-1am daily; Ⓜ Akropoli)

Local Life
Street Snacks

Since 1910 **Ariston** (☎210 322 7626; Voulis 10, Syntagma; pies €1.40-2; ⏱10am-4pm Mon-Fri; Ⓜ Syntagma) has been baking the best fresh *tyropites* (cheese pies), the perfect snack on the run. Try its renowned *kourou* (thick type of pastry) variety or one of the many other tasty fillings, such as red peppers, mushrooms, chicken or spinach.

Platanos

TAVERNA €

14 | Map p62, B4

This village-style taverna with tables under the giant plane tree in the courtyard is popular among Greeks and tourists. It serves delicious home-style fare, such as oven-baked potatoes, lamb fricassee and beef with quince and summer greens. (☎210 322 0666; Diogenous 4, Plaka; mains €7-9; ⏱lunch & dinner daily; Ⓜ Monastiraki)

Doris

TAVERNA €

15 | Map p62, C1

This Athens institution started as a *galaktopoleio* (dairy store) in 1947 and became a traditional *mayirio* catering to city workers. Pink walls aside, the classic marble tables, historical photos and old-style waiters give it a yesteryear ambience. Choose from the trays of daily specials, as the printed English menu only has the basics. Finish off with renowned *loukoumadhes* (ball-shaped doughnuts with honey and cinnamon). (☎210 323 2671; Praxitelous 30, Syntagma; mains €4-9; ⏱8am-6.30pm Mon-Sat; Ⓜ Panepistimio)

Filema

MEZEDHES €

16 | Map p62, C2

This popular *mezedhopoleio* has two shopfronts and fills tables on both sides of the narrow street, which is a busy commercial area by day but a peaceful spot when the shops close. It has a great range of mezedhes such as plump *keftedhes* (small, tasty rissoles) and grilled sardines. (☎210 325 0222;

Romvis 16, Syntagma; mains €7.50-10, mezedhes €3.50-6.50; ⏱lunch & dinner Mon-Sat, noon-8pm Sun; Ⓜ Syntagma)

Pure Bliss
CAFE €

17 Map p62, C2

Enjoy the laid-back vibe at one of the few places in Athens where you can get organic fair-trade coffee, exotic teas and soy products. There's a range of healthy salads, sandwiches, smoothies and mostly organic food, wine and cocktails. (📞210 325 0360; www.purebliss.gr; Romvis 24a, Syntagma; items €3-9; ⏱10am-1am Mon-Sat, 5-9pm Sun; 📶; Ⓜ Syntagma)

Palia Taverna Tou Psara
TAVERNA, SEAFOOD €€

18 Map p62, B4

Away from the main hustle and bustle of Plaka, this taverna is a cut above the rest, which is why it fills the tables on the street, the terrace and the place next door. There is a choice of mezedhes but it is known as the best seafood taverna in Plaka (top fresh fish €65 per kilogram). (📞210 321 8734; www.psaras-taverna.gr; Erehtheos 16, Plaka; mains €12-24; ⏱11am-12.30pm Wed-Mon; Ⓜ Akropoli)

Drinking

Seven Jokers
BAR

19 Map p62, E2

This small, friendly bar right in central Athens is a good place for a coffee

National Historical Museum (p67)

by day or a quiet early drink, then the vibe steps up several notches way into the night. It anchors a party block so Athenians come here for a reliably lively night out. (Voulis 7, Syntagma; Ⓜ Syntagma)

Baba Au Rum
BAR

20 Map p62, C2

Fab cocktail mixologists concoct the tipple of your dreams, and the non-smoking policy is usually enforced indoors. (Klitiou 6, Syntagma; Ⓜ Syntagma)

Bartessera
BAR

21 Map p62, D2

Tucked at the end of a narrow arcade off Kolokotroni, with a quirky central

Local Life

Party Central

Seek out the area around **Plateia Karytsi** and **Kolokotroni**, for crowds of Athenians out on the town. You'll find old favourites like **Toy** (Karytsi 10, Syntagma; M Syntagma), where locals gather for coffee by day and glam cocktails by night. But remember, Greeks start late: bars start hopping after midnight.

there's a theatre upstairs. (211 400 0863; www.boozecooperativa.com; Kolokotroni 57, Syntagma; 10am-late Mon-Fri, from 3pm Sat, from noon Sun; ; M Monastiraki)

Brettos

BAR, DISTILLERY

24 Map p62, C5

A Plaka landmark, this quaint bar has a stunning backlit wall of coloured bottles, old wine barrels and an authentic old-fashioned character. It's a quiet spot for a night- (or day-) cap, with a tempting range of homemade wine, ouzo, brandy and other spirits to imbibe or take away. (Kydathineon 41, Plaka; M Akropoli)

courtyard, this friendly place is a little oasis by day and a lively bar at night, with a hip 30-something crowd, guest DJs and art exhibitions. (Kolokotroni 25, Syntagma; M Syntagma)

Galaxy Bar

BAR

22 Map p62, E1

Not to be confused with the Hilton's sky bar of the same name, this sweet little wood-panelled place has a homey saloon feel. It's traditionally been an old-time drinking hole for professionals, politicans and lawyers. (Stadiou 10, Syntagma; Mon-Sat; M Syntagma)

Booze Cooperativa

CAFE, BAR

23 Map p62, C1

By day, this gay-friendly laid-back arty hang-out is full of hip young Athenians playing chess and backgammon and working on their Macs on the 6m-long table; later it transforms into a happening bar that rocks till late. The basement hosts art exhibitions and

Barley Cargo

BEER BAR

25 Map p62, D1

This fantastic beer bar offers over 150 different versions of the sweet elixir, many of them from Greek microbreweries. Or sip a trappist ale at one of the wooden barrel tables or in the crowds spilling into the street. (210 323 0445; Kolokotroni 6, Syntagma; M Syntagma)

Kimolia Art Cafe

CAFE

26 Map p62, E4

Painted bright, pretty colours, this tiny cafe with marble floors and windows looking onto the street offers a full range of sandwiches and coffee and tea drinks. It also does a breakfast spread (€6 to €10). (Iperidou 5, Plaka; 9am-1am; ; M Syntagma)

Klepsydra
CAFE

27 Map p62, A4

Tucked away in a delightfully quiet spot under the Acropolis, with shady outdoor tables and friendly service, Klepsydra is a favourite with locals and an ideal rest spot after serious sightseeing; there's a small selection of snacks, such as *spanakopites* (spinach pies). (☏210 321 4152; Klepsydras, Plaka; snacks €4; ⏰8.30am-1.30am daily; Ⓜ Monastiraki)

Entertainment

Perivoli Tou Ouranou
MUSIC TAVERNA

28 ⭐ Map p62, E5

A favourite Plaka music haunt in a rustic old-style venue where you can have dinner and listen to authentic *laïka* (urban popular music) and *rembetika* by leading exponents. (☏210 323 5517; Lysikratous 19, Plaka; ⏰9pm-late Thu-Sun; Ⓜ Akropoli, Syntagma)

Local Life
The Booze Market

When you're in town, check the website for the **Booze Market** (http://theboozemarket.blogspot.gr; ⏰Sep-May) or email, to see if one's on. It's a collective of local arts, crafts and design frequented by some of the city's most creative young artists. Find everything from handmade jewellery to sculpture.

Cine Paris
CINEMA

29 ⭐ Map p62, D5

A magical place to see a movie, this traditional old rooftop cinema in Plaka has great views of the Acropolis from some seats. (☏210 322 0721; Kydathineon 22, Plaka; Ⓜ Syntagma)

Palea Plakiotiki Taverna Stamatopoulos
MUSIC TAVERNA

30 ⭐ Map p62, B4

This Plaka institution with live music nightly fills up late with locals; arrive early for a table. (☏210 322 8722; www.stamatopoulostavern.gr; Lyssiou 26, Plaka; ⏰7pm-2am Mon-Sat, 11am-2am Sun; Ⓜ Monastiraki)

Mostrou
MUSIC TAVERNA

31 ⭐ Map p62, B4

Popular full-sized stage and dance floor; in summer, there's more sedate live music on the terrace. (☏210 322 5558; Mnisikleous 22, cnr Lyssiou, Plaka; ⏰7pm-2am Mon-Sat, 11am-2am Sun; Ⓜ Monastiraki)

Shopping

Aidini
ARTS & CRAFTS

32 🔒 Map p62, E4

Artisan Errikos Aidini's unique metal creations are made in his workshop at the back of this charming store, including small mirrors, candlesticks, lamps, planes and his signature bronze boats. (📞210 323 4591; Nikis 32, Plaka; Ⓜ Syntagma)

Apriati

JEWELLERY

33 Map p62, E2

The main branch of this delightful store has a tempting selection of fun and original contemporary designs from Athena Axioti, Themis Bobolas and other local designers. There's another store on Pendelis and one in Kolonaki. (📞210 322 9183; www.apriati. com; Stadiou 3, Syntagma; Ⓜ Syntagma)

Lalaounis

JEWELLERY

34 Map p62, F2

Leading Greek jeweller Lalaounis' exquisitely crafted creations reflect

☑ Top Tip

One-Stop Shopping

Big Greek chains combine lots of wares under one roof. The enormous **Attica** (📞211 180 2500; Panepistimiou 7, Syntagma; ⊙10am-9pm Mon-Fri, to 7pm Sat; Ⓜ Syntagma) department store has it all, **Folli-Follie** (📞210 323 0601; www.folli-follie.com; Ermou 37, Syntagma; Ⓜ Syntagma) carries jewellery and accessories, **Eleftheroudakis** (📞210 331 4180; Panepistimiou 17, Syntagma; Ⓜ Syntagma) is a bibliophile heaven and **Public** (📞210 324 6210; Plateia Syntagmatos, Syntagma; 📶; Ⓜ Syntagma) specialises in computers, stationery and books. **Ermou street** is lined with major chains.

ancient Greek motifs and draw inspiration from other cultures, biology, nature and mythology. (📞210 361 1371; Panepistimiou 6 , cnr Voukourestiou, Syntagma; Ⓜ Syntagma)

Cellier

WINE

35 Map p62, F2

A delectable collection of some of Greece's best wines and liqueurs, with knowledgable staff to explain Greek varieties and winemakers, and boxed gift packs. (📞210 361 0040; Kriezotou 1, Syntagma; Ⓜ Syntagma)

Amorgos

HANDICRAFTS

36 Map p62, D4

Charming store crammed with Greek folk art, trinkets, ceramics, embroidery and wood-carved furniture made by the owner. (📞210 324 3836; www. amorgosart.gr; Kodrou 3, Plaka; Ⓜ Syntagma)

Zoumboulakis Gallery

ART

37 Map p62, G2

An excellent range of limited-edition prints and posters by leading Greek artists, including Tsarouhis, Mytara and Fassianos. (📞210 363 4454; www. zoumboulakis.gr; Kriezotou 6, Syntagma; Ⓜ Syntagma)

Ekavi

BOARDGAMES

38 Map p62, D3

If you're hooked on the local sport, there's a huge selection of backgammon boards, as well as great chess pieces depicting the battles of Troy, the Ottomans vs the Byzantines and other themes. (☎210 323 7740; www. manopoulos.com; Mitropoleos 36, Syntagma; ⓂSyntagma)

Zolotas
JEWELLERY

39 🔒 Map p62, E2

Internationally renowned Zolotas breathes life into ancient Greece with replicas of museum pieces, having had the exclusive rights to make copies of the real thing since 1972. (☎210 331 3320; Stadiou 9, Syntagma; ⓂSyntagma)

Xylouris
MUSIC

40 🔒 Map p62, D1

This music treasure trove is run by the son and widow of Cretan legend Nikos Xylouris. Georgios is a font of music knowledge and can guide you through the comprehensive range of traditional and contemporary Greek music, including select and rare recordings, and eclectic world music. Also a branch at Museum of Greek Popular Instruments (p67). (☎210 322 2711; www.xilouris.gr; Arcade, Panepistimiou 39, Panepistimio; ⓂSyntagma)

Anavasi
BOOKS

41 🔒 Map p62, D3

This travel bookshop carries an extensive range of Greece maps, and walking and activity guides. Its 2012

Zoumboulakis Gallery

Attiki-Voiotia map (€8) also has suggestions for excursions and walks. (☎210 321 8104; www.anavasi.gr; Voulis 32, Apollonos, Syntagma; ⏱9.30am-5.30pm Mon & Wed , to 8.30pm Tue, Thu & Fri, 10am-3pm Sat; ⓂSyntagma)

Archipelagos
JEWELLERY

42 🔒 Map p62, C5

Unique contemporary pieces in silver and gold for jewellery lovers with moderate budgets. There are also interesting ceramics and trinkets, including fine silver bookmarks. (☎210 323 1321; Adrianou 142, Plaka; ⓂAkropoli)

Explore

Benaki Museum & Kolonaki

Kolonaki is an adjective as much as a place: it's the suburb that most epitomises the Athenian elite. Undeniably chic, it's where old money mixes with new. Named after an obscure column in the central Plateia Kolonakiou (Kolonaki Sq), Kolonaki stretches from Syntagma to the foothills of Lykavittos Hill, and is home to popular cafes, restaurants, galleries, museums, boutiques and stylish apartment blocks.

The Sights in a Day

☀ Watch the world go by while fuelling up with coffee on Plateia Kolonakiou or at nearby **Filion** (p85). Once you're sated, head out to three of the best museums in Athens: the **Museum of Cycladic Art** (p82), the **Byzantine & Christian Museum** (p82), and the **Benaki Museum** (p76). These could easily fill your day.

☀ Plan to lunch at the Benaki with its terrace cafe, refreshing garden and Acropolis views. Then the browsing begins. Kolonaki is the romping area of fashionistas, so if haute couture is what you're after, you've come to the right place. Even just visiting **Fanourakis** (p86), the stellar jeweller, or **Vassilis Zoulias** (p87), the couturier, will thrill. Or simply cruise the streets, window-shopping and watching Athenians do their thing.

☾ Plan to dine out at one of the local Italian restaurants such as **Capanna** (p85) or **Il Postino** (p85), or people-watch at **Kalamaki Kolonaki** (p84). Then join the fray at the bars and clubs, like those on Plateia Kolonakiou, Ploutarhou street or pedestrianised Haritos street, such as **City** (p85).

For a local's day in Kolonaki, see p78.

Top Sights

Benaki Museum (p76)

○ Local Life

People-Watching in Kolonaki (p78)

♥ Best of Athens

Museums

Benaki Museum (p76)

Museum of Cycladic Art (p82)

Byzantine & Christian Museum (p82)

National Art Gallery (p83)

Theocharakis Foundation for the Fine Arts & Music (p83)

Cafes

Da Capo (p78)

Filion (p85)

Petite Fleur (p85)

To Tsai (p85)

Getting There

Ⓜ **Metro** Emerge at Evangelismos station (blue line) for the eastern extents of Kolonaki.

Ⓜ **Metro** Syntagma station (blue and red lines) brings you to Kolonaki's western edge.

Top Sights
Benaki Museum

Greece's finest private museum contains the vast collection of Antonis Benakis, accumulated during 35 years of avid collecting in Europe and Asia. In 1931 he turned the family house into a museum and presented it to the Greek nation. The collection displays an astounding breadth: Bronze Age finds from Mycenae and Thessaly; works by El Greco; ecclesiastical furniture brought from Asia Minor; pottery, copper, silver and woodwork from Egypt, Asia Minor and Mesopotamia; and a stunning collection of Greek regional costumes.

👁 Map p80, C5

www.benaki.gr

Koumbari 1, cnr Leoforos Vasilissis Sofias, Kolonaki

adult/child €7/free

🕑 9am-5pm Wed, Fri & Sat, to midnight Thu, to 3pm Sun

Ⓜ Syntagma

Benaki Museum

Don't Miss

Earliest Finds

Make sure you pass by the cases in room 1 on the ground floor to see flint flakes from the Middle Paleolithic period: at 50,000–40,000 BC they may be the oldest man-made thing you ever see.

Ground Floor: Hordes of Treasure

Take your time on the ground floor, where priceless displays range from inscribed golden tablets to Byzantine mosaics, fragile Coptic tapestries, Mycenaean gold jewellery, regal funerary urns and 6th-century gold bracelets from Cyprus.

Costumes

On the 1st floor, prepare to be wowed by a seemingly endless sequence of native dress, from islands all over Greece and on into the Peloponnese, Epiros, Macedonia and Thrace. The spacious displays are interspersed with other priceless objects, like carved marble door frames and Ottoman jewel-encrusted crowns.

Reception Halls

Amazingly, Benaki collected entire rooms: inlaid ceilings, marble floors, antique benches. Two particularly striking examples are the reception hall of the Voulgaris Manision in Hydra (a gift of Pasha Gazi-Hassam) and a mid-18th-century hall from Kazani, Macedonia.

Cretan School Painters

Painters in Venetian-held Crete (15th–16th centuries) developed a signature icon-painting style. The Benaki holds masterpieces of the genre in room 12, which includes work by Domenikos Theotokopoulos (El Greco, 1541–1614), and several by Theodoros Poulakis (1622–1692), in room 27.

☑ Top Tips

▶ The Benaki has expanded into several branches to house its vast, diverse collections, which host a full schedule of rotating exhibitions, posted on its website.

▶ The Benaki Museum Pireos Annexe (p129) in an impressive former industrial building is tops for art.

▶ Museum of Islamic Art (p129) holds a top-notch collection.

▶ N. Hadjikyriakos-Ghika Gallery offers insight into the great artist's life and work.

✕ Take a Break

The Benaki's **cafe** (mains €12-16; Ⓜ Evangelismos) is renowned for great food in an open dining room, stretching out onto a terrace overlooking the national gardens and the Acropolis. Locals often come to the museum just for lunch!

Otherwise, pop over to Plateia Kolonakiou to a cafe like Da Capo (p78).

Local Life
People-Watching in Kolonaki

On Plateia Kolonakiou you'll find the original people-watching cafes teeming with yuppies, actors, politicians, journalists and a passing parade of aristocratic old Athenian ladies, style queens and glitzy fashion victims. The cool younger set frequent the bars on Skoufa, Haritos and Ploutarhou. Join the flow for what Kolonaki has always been – solid, good fun and ever-fashionable.

1 Coffee Klatch

An absolute pastime in Kolonaki is the extended people-perusing coffee session. Try iconic **Da Capo** (Tsakalof 1, Kolonaki; Syntagma), which anchors the cafes on the main square and is *the* place to be seen. (It's self-serve if you can find a table.)

2 Designer Shopping

Kolonaki is Athens' boutique epicentre. Fashionistas and dreamers love

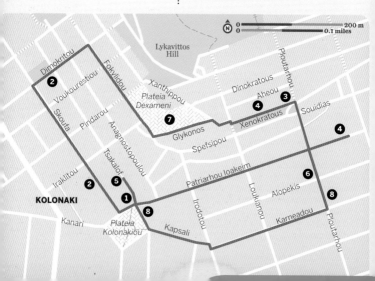

Luisa (☎ 210 363 5600; Skoufa 17, Kolonaki; Ⓜ Syntagma) for its A-list international couturiers. Or go totally Greek and totally natural at **Parthenis** (☎ 210 363 3158; www.orsalia-parthenis.gr; Dimokritou 20, cnr Tsakalof, Kolonaki; Ⓜ Syntagma), where a father-and-daughter team offer classic-silhouettes in natural fibers.

❸ Traditional Taverna

Filippou (☎ 210 721 6390; Xenokratous 19; mains €8-12; ☺ lunch & dinner, closed Sat night & Sun; Ⓜ Evangelismos) is always packed with locals enjoying the re-nowned home-style fare that this clas-sic taverna has been dishing out since 1923. White-linen covered tables spill into the courtyard, but book ahead to ensure you'll get one.

❹ Art Galleries

Join art connoisseurs at Kolonaki's galleries. **Xippas Gallery** (☎ 210 331 9333; Patriarhou Ioakeim 53, Kolonaki; ☺ Tue-Sat; Ⓜ Evangelismos) shows international contemporary art's rising stars (also in Paris and Geneva), while **Medusa Art Gallery** (☎ 210 724 4552; www.medusaart gallery.com; Xenokratous 7, Kolonaki; Ⓜ Evan-gelismos) has focused for over 30 years on excellent Greek contemporary painting, sculpture, installations and photography.

❺ Cool Off with Fro-Yo

Kolonaki's newest trend: frozen Greek yogurt. And at **Yozen** (☎ 210 360 3196; Tsakalof 7, Kolonaki; frozen yogurt from €3; ☺ 11am-late; Ⓜ Syntagma) it's totally deli-cious...flavours range from undoctored pure yogurt to a rotating menu of fruit, chocolate and other inspirations. Homemade spoon sweets and the standard range of candy bits serve as toppings.

❻ Super Streetside Dinner

Watch the jet-set head out for the night, streetside at **Oikeio** (☎ 210 725 9216; Ploutarhou 15, Kolonaki; specials €7-13; ☺ 1pm-2.30am Mon-Sat; Ⓜ Evangelismos). With excellent home-style cooking, this modern taverna lives up to its name (meaning 'homey'). It's decorated like a cosy bistro on the inside, and tables on the pavement allow people-watching without the normal Kolonaki bill. Book ahead, as it always fills up.

❼ Cinema Under the Stars

Things in Kolonaki get more sedate in the streets towards Lykavitos. The classic open-air cinema, **Dexameni** (☎ 210 362 3942; Plateia Dexameni, Kolonaki; Ⓜ Evangelismos), is in a lovely spot up on Plateia Dexameni, with a wall of cascading bougainvillea, deck chairs and little tables to rest your beer on.

❽ Dress to Kill

Join the beautiful young things at **Rock'n'Roll** (☎ 210 721 7127; Plateia Kolonakiou; Ⓜ Evangelismos), a Kolonaki classic, that lives up to its name. Satur-day afternoon dance parties get wild, and each night has different DJ-ed sets. Or head to **Mai Tai** (Ploutarhou 18; Ⓜ Evangelismos), where Kolonaki's best dressed pack into the narrow bar until they spill out into the street.

4 Lykavittos Hill

Lykavittos Hill

0 ————— 200 m
N 0 ————— 0.1 miles

Athineon Efivon
Karahristou
Dimoharous
Dinokratous

For reviews see

Top Sights	p76
Sights	p82
Eating	p84
Drinking	p85
Entertainment	p86
Shopping	p86

Hoida
Aristodimou
Iroflou

Doras D'Istria

Aristippou

Kleomenous

Dinokratous

Xenokratous

Plateia
Dante

Evzonon

Aheou

Xenokratous

Souidias

Genadiou I

Iasiou

Monis Petraki

12
11
Haritos

Patera I

Ravine

22

Patriarhou Ioakeim

Marasli

Evangelismos
Hospital

Ypsilandou

Alopekis

Ploutarhou

19 9

Karneadou

Loukianou

Plateia
Megalis tou
Genous Sholi

Leof Vasilissis Sofias

Ventiri K

Ypsilandou

M

Evangelismos

M

Leof Vasileos Alexandrou

Hilton

Vasilissis Sofias

Leof Vas Konstantinou

Rizari

3
National
Art Gallery

Byzantine &
Christian
Museum

1

Mihalakopoulou

Plateia
Madritis Vrasida

8

Sights

Byzantine & Christian Museum
RELIGIOUS ART MUSEUM

1 Map p80, E5

This outstanding museum – on the grounds of former Villa Ilissia, an urban oasis – presents a priceless collection of Christian art from the 3rd to 20th centuries. Thematic snapshots of the Byzantine and post-Byzantine world are exceptionally presented in expansive well-lit multilevel galleries, clearly arranged chronologically with English translations. The collection includes icons, frescoes, sculptures, textiles, manuscripts, vestments and mosaics. (☎210 721 1027; www.byzantine museum.gr; Leoforos Vasilissis Sofias 22, Kolonaki; adult/child €4/free; ◷9am-4pm Tue-Sun; Ⓜ Evangelismos)

Museum of Cycladic Art
ARCHAEOLOGICAL MUSEUM

2 Map p80, D5

This exceptional private museum boasts the biggest independent collection of distinctive Cycladic art and holds excellent periodic exhibitions. The 1st-floor Cycladic collection, dating from 3000 BC to 2000 BC, includes the marble figurines that inspired many 20th-century artists, such as Picasso and Modigliani, with their simplicity and purity of form. The

---

Understand
Byzantine Athens

With the rise of the Byzantine Empire, which blended Hellenistic culture with Christianity, the Greek city of Byzantium (renamed Constantinople in AD 330, present-day İstanbul) became the capital of the Roman Empire headed by the Roman Emperor Constantine I, a Christian convert. While Rome went into terminal decline, this eastern capital began to grow in wealth and strength as a Christian state. In the ensuing centuries Byzantine Greece faced continued pressure from the Persians and Arabs, but it retained its hold over the region.

Christianity was made the official religion of Greece in AD 394, and worship of Greek and Roman gods was banned. Athens remained an important cultural centre until AD 529, when the teaching of 'pagan' classical philosophy was forbidden in favour of Christian theology. From 1200 to 1450 Athens was occupied by a succession of opportunistic invaders – Franks, Catalans, Florentines and Venetians. By the time it was chosen as the new Greek capital in 1834, it was little more than a dusty outpost of the Byzantine Empire.

The Byzantine Empire outlived Rome, lasting until the Turks captured Constantinople in 1453.

rest of the museum features Greek and Cypriot art dating from 2000 BC to the 4th century AD. (📞210 722 8321; www.cycladic.gr; Neofytou Douka 4, cnr Leoforos Vasilissis Sofias, Kolonaki; adult/child €7/free; ⏰10am-5pm Mon, Wed, Fri & Sat, to 8pm Thu, 11am-5pm Sun; Ⓜ Evangelismos)

National Art Gallery ART MUSEUM

3 ◎ Map p80, G5

This rich collection of Greek art spans four centuries. The newer wing houses its permanent collection and traces the key art movements chronologically. The 1st floor includes the post-Byzantine period, the gallery's prized El Greco paintings, including *The Crucifixion* and *Symphony of the Angels,* and works from the Ionian period until 1900. The 2nd floor holds leading 20th-century artists. Works by European masters include paintings by Picasso. It hosts major international exhibitions. (📞210 723 5857; www.nationalgallery.gr; Leoforos Vasileos Konstantinou 50, Kolonaki; adult/child €6.50/free; ⏰9am-3pm Mon & Wed-Sat, 10am-2pm Sun; Ⓜ Evangelismos)

Lykavittos Hill LANDMARK, PARK

4 ◎ Map p80, F1

Lykavittos means 'Hill of Wolves' and derives from ancient times when the hill was surrounded by countryside and its pine-covered slopes were inhabited by wolves. A path leads to the summit from the top of Loukianou for the finest panoramas of the city and the Attic basin – the *nefos* (pollu-

Lykavittos Hill

tion haze) permitting. Alternatively, take the **funicular railway** (📞210 721 0701; return €6; ⏰9am-3am, half-hourly), or *teleferik,* from the top of Ploutarhou in Kolonaki. Perched on the summit is the little **Chapel of Agios Georgios**, floodlit like a beacon over the city at night. (Ⓜ Evangelismos)

Theocharakis Foundation for the Fine Arts & Music GALLERY

5 ◎ Map p80, B5

This excellent centre, in a restored neoclassical building, has three levels of exhibition space featuring local and international 20th- and 21st-century artists, a theatre, an art shop and a pleasant cafe with wi-fi. Music performances are held between Sep-

tember and May. (☎210 361 1206; www.
thf.gr; Leoforos Vasilissis Sofias 9, Kolonaki;
adult/child €6/free; ⏰10am-6pm Mon, Wed &
Fri-Sun, to 10pm Thu; Ⓜ Syntagma)

Skoufa Gallery   GALLERY

6 Map p80, C4

A long-standing anchor of contemporary Greek artists just off Plateia
Kolinakiou. (☎210 364 3025; www.skoufa
gallery.gr; Skoufa 4, Kolonaki; ⏰Tue-Sat;
Ⓜ Syntagma)

CAN   ART GALLERY

7 Map p80, C2

The brainchild of Christina Androuli-
daki, this new entrant on the Kolonaki
scene is building a stable of emerging
contemporary Greek artists to show.
(☎210 339 0833; www.can-gallery.com;
Anagnostopoulou 42, Kolonaki; ⏰11am-3pm &
5pm-8pm Tue-Fri, 11am-4pm Sat, closed Aug;
Ⓜ Syntagma)

Eating

Alatsi   CRETAN €€

8 Map p80, H5

Cretan food is in. Alatsi represents
the new breed of trendy upscale
restaurants, serving traditional Cretan
cuisine, such as *gamopilafo* (wedding
pilaf) with lamb or rare *stamna-
gathi* (wild greens), to fashionable
Athenians. The food and service are
excellent. (☎210 721 0501; Vrasida 13, Ilissia; mains €12-16.50; Ⓜ Evangelismos)

Ouzadiko   MEZEDHES €€

9 Map p80, E4

The basement location in the Lemos
Centre lets it down, but Ouzadiko is
nonetheless cosy and renowned for its
refined regional mezedhes and huge
range of Greek dishes, washed down
with an ouzo or two from its extensive
selection. In summer, tables fill an interior courtyard. Bookings advisable.
(☎210 729 5484; Karneadou 25-29, Kolonaki;
mains €10-17; ⏰lunch & dinner Tue-Sat, lunch
Sun; Ⓜ Evangelismos)

Papadakis   SEAFOOD €€€

10 Map p80, C2

This elegant restaurant specialises in
creative seafood, like stewed octopus
with honey and sweet wine, *salatouri*
(fish salad) and sea salad (a type of
green seaweed/sea asparagus). Service
can be snooty. (☎210 360 8621; Fokylidou
15, Kolonaki; mains €18-38; ⏰Mon-Sat;
Ⓜ Syntagma)

Capanna ITALIAN €€

11 Map p80, E3

One of Kolonaki's newest restaurants, Capanna hugs a corner, tables wrapping around the sidewalk in summer. Cuisine is fresh Italian, from enormous pizza pies to gnocchi with gorgonzola. Hearty eating with attentive service and a goblet of wine. (☑210 724 1777; Ploutarhou 38 & Haritos 42, Kolonaki; mains €10-17; ☺1pm-1am Tue-Sun; Ⓜ Evangelismos)

Kavatza TAVERNA €

12 Map p80, E3

Straight, value-for-money Greek dishes. Look at what's fresh behind the counter. (☑210 724 1862; Spefsipou 10, Kolonaki; mains €4-8; Ⓜ Evangelismos)

Il Postino ITALIAN €

13 Map p80, A1

Some consider this the best downhome Italian food in Athens. In the mood for a plate of home-made gnocchi with pesto (€12) before a night out clubbing? Sneak into this little side street and sup under old photos of Roma. (☑210 364 1414; Grivaion 3, Kolonaki; pasta €8-12; Ⓜ Panepistimio)

Nice N' Easy CAFE €

14 Map p80, B2

Dig into organic, fresh sandwiches, salads and brunch treats like *huevos rancheros* beneath images of Louis Armstrong and Marilyn Monroe.

(☑210 361 7201; www.niceneasy.gr; Omirou 60, Kolonaki; sandwiches €5-10; ☺lunch & dinner daily, breakfast Sat & Sun; Ⓜ Panepistimio)

Drinking

Filion CAFE

15 Map p80, B3

Set up shop here to find the intellectual set: artists, writers and filmmakers. (Skoufa 34, Kolonaki; Ⓜ Syntagma)

Petite Fleur CAFE

16 Map p80, B3

Petite Fleur serves up large mugs of hot chocolate and speciality cappucinos in a quiet, almost-Parisian ambience. (Omirou 44; Ⓜ Panepistimio)

To Tsai TEA HOUSE

17 Map p80, A3

Get a Zen vibe as you sip tea at natural wood tables, and on a lively day, a

Local Life
Haritos Street

One of the best bars on the hopping pedestrianised end of Haritos, **City** (Haritos 43; Ⓜ Evangelismos) makes an excellent *mastiha* cocktail. It's a popular spot for the younger set: most nights there are patrons spilling out on to the road, drinking on the steps of the apartment blocks opposite.

bit of Dixieland jazz will be tinkling in the background. This inviting tea shop also offers light meals (€6 to €8), such as soup or grilled chicken. (☏210 338 8941; Alexandrou Soutsou 19, Kolonaki; ⌚6am-9pm Mon-Sat, daily in winter; Ⓜ Syntagma)

Mommy
BAR

18 Map p80, A1

Further along and tucked way back in a side street, Mommy is popular with English-speaking locals and for its weekly '80s night. (Delfon 4; Ⓜ Panepistimiou)

Doors
BAR

19 🚇 Map p80, E4

Drop in for dinner theatre on weekdays, and drinks every night. Doors is next to **La Boom**, an '80s disco that moves to the beach in summer. (Karneadou 25-29; Ⓜ Evangelismos)

Frame Garden
BAR, RESTAURANT

20 Map p80, D3

In summer you can chill out with a cocktail on the comfy lounges in the verdant garden of Plateia Dexameni, opposite the main restaurant in the up-scale St George Lykavittos Hotel. The new young chef offers a seasonal menu of creative Mediterranean dishes. (☏210 741 6000; Dinokratous 1, Kolonaki; mains €16-22; ⌚lunch & dinner daily May-Oct; Ⓜ Evangelismos)

Entertainment

Baraki Tou Vasili
LIVE MUSIC

21 ⭐ Map p80, B2

An intimate, friendly live-music venue renowned for giving a break to an eclectic line-up of up-and-comers, and occasional touring artists. (☏210 362 3625; Didotou 3, Kolonaki; ⌚10.30pm-3am, closed Jun-Sep; Ⓜ Panepistimio)

Shopping

Fanourakis
JEWELLERY

22 Map p80, E4

One of the most creative, exciting Greek jewellers, Fanourakis designs delicate pieces of folded gold, encrusted rings, bows, and other unique creations. The distinctive forms are sheer art, a factor that is also reflected in the prices, though it now has a more inexpensive line as well. (☏210 721 1762;

🔍 Local Life
Shoes!

Kolonaki = shoes. Shoe fetishists love the colours and styles to blow the imagination and budget at **Kalogirou** (☏210 722 8804; Patriarhou Ioakeim 4, Kolonaki; Ⓜ Evangelismos). Others swear that **Prasini** (☏210 364 1590; Tsakalof 7-9, Kolonaki; Ⓜ Evangelismos) is shoe heaven, with French, Italian, Spanish and Greek designer footwear for the really well-heeled.

www.fanourakis.gr; Patriarhou Ioakeim 23, Kolonaki; M Syntagma)

Apivita
COSMETICS

23 🔒 Map p80, B3

Apivita's flagship store has the full range of its excellent natural beauty products and an express spa downstairs for pampering on the run. (📞 210 364 0760; www.apivita.com; Solonos 26, Kolonaki; M Syntagma)

Vassilis Zoulias
CLOTHING, SHOES

24 🔒 Map p80, A3

An exquisite range of elegant, feminine shoes can be found at the boutique store of Greece's Manolo Blahnik. Some of these designs are works of art inspired by '50s and '60s films, as are his couture line. (📞 210 361 4762; www.vassiliszoulias.com; Akademias 30, Kolonaki; M Syntagma)

Elena Votsi
JEWELLERY

25 🔒 Map p80, D4

Votsi is renowned for her original, big and bold designs using exquisite semiprecious stones, which sell in New York and London. Her profile was boosted when she was chosen to design the 2004 Olympic Games medal. (📞 210 360 0936; www.elenavotsi. com; Xanthou 7, Kolonaki; M Evangelismos)

Goutis
ANTIQUES

26 🔒 Map p80, B3

Packed into this tiny treasure-trove of a store you'll find an eclectic

Shoe shopping at Vassilis Zoulias

collection of antiques and collectables, mostly from Greece and France, including jewellery worn with traditional dress, prints, silverware, royal crockery and embroideries. (📞 210 361 3557; Dimokritou 10, Kolonaki; M Syntagma)

Bettina
CLOTHING

27 🔒 Map p80, C3

This mod boutique carries top-name fashion, including creations by Greek fashion queen Sophia Kokosalaki, Angelos Frentzos and other well-known local and international designers. (📞 210 339 2094; www.bettina.com.gr; Anagnostopoulou 29, Kolonaki; M Syntagma)

Explore

Temple of Olympian Zeus & Panathenaic Stadium

To the east of the Acropolis, the Zappeio Gardens and the ruins of the Temple of Olympian Zeus lead to the elegant Panathenaic Stadium, built into Ardettos Hill. The attractive residential district Mets, characterised by delightful neoclassical and prewar houses, runs up and behind the stadium. Northeast of Mets, Pangrati is a diverse neighbourhood with interesting music clubs, cafes and old-style tavernas.

The Sights in a Day

☀ Take a gander at the enormous **Temple of Olympian Zeus** (p90), which took over 700 years to build, and read Hadrian's inscription on nearby **Hadrian's Arch** (p91), then head over to the spectacular marble **Panathenaic Stadium** (p94) to see the site of the first modern Olympics.

☀ Unwind under the shade trees with Athens' best pizza at **Colibri** (p96), then walk it off at **Athens' First Cemetery** (p94), where Greek luminaries are buried in elaborate tombs. Or seek your repose at the lush **Zappeio Gardens** (p95) and nosh on simple dishes at its **Aigli Cafe** (p97).

☾ Dinner will be a challenge: choose between the authentic Greek **Aigli Restaurant** (p96), the modern Greek fusion **Cucina Povera** (p96), with its excellent wine list, or perhaps Athens' very best restaurant: **Spondi** (p95), with a French twist. Finish the night out with live music at Athens' premier jazz venue, the **Half Note Jazz Club** (p97), or catch more eclectic tunes at **Cafe Alavastron** (p97). Alternatively, watch a movie under the stars at the **Aigli Cinema** (p97).

For a local's day in Pangrati, see p96.

👁 Top Sights

Temple of Olympian Zeus (p90)

💜 Best of Athens

Food

Spondi (p95)

Cucina Povera (p96)

Colibri (p96)

Entertainment

Half Note Jazz Club (p97)

Cafe Alavastron (p97)

Aigli Cinema (p97)

Getting There

Ⓜ **Metro** To reach Temple of Olympian Zeus use the Akropoli station (red line) or, closer to Zappeio Gardens, the Syntagma station (blue and red lines).

🚌 **Trolleybus** To get as close to Pangrati or Mets as possible take trolleybus 2, 4 or 11. Or walk over from the metro – about 15 minutes.

Top Sights
Temple of Olympian Zeus

You can't miss this striking marvel, smack in the centre of Athens. Also known as the Olympeion, it is the largest temple in Greece and, as the name suggests, was dedicated to the supreme god Zeus. Peisistratos began building the temple in the 6th century BC on the western bank of the Ilissos River, but construction stalled due to a lack of funds. A succession of leaders tried to finish the job; Hadrian finally completed the task in AD 131.

◉ Map p92, A2

☑ 210 922 6330

adult/child €2/free, with Acropolis pass free

◷ 8am-3pm

Ⓜ Syntagma, Akropoli

Temple of Olympian Zeus

Don't Miss

Temple

The colossal Temple of Olympian Zeus took more than 700 years to build. When Hadrian finally completed it in AD 131 he put one of the largest statues in the world – a giant gold and ivory statue of Zeus – in the *cella* and, in typically immodest fashion, placed an equally large one of himself next to it. The temple was pillaged by Barbarian invaders in the the 3rd century AD and later fell into disuse.

Columns

The temple is impressive for the sheer size of its 104 Corinthian columns – 17m high with a base diameter of 1.7m – of which 15 remain. Imagine the whole array and you'll get an idea of how grand a site this was. The fallen column was blown down in a gale in 1852.

Original Temple

The Olympeion is built on the site of a smaller temple (590–560 BC), which was dedicated to the cult of Olympian Zeus. Look closely: its foundations can still be seen on the site.

Hadrian's Arch

Just alongside the Temple, and free to peruse, sits a lofty monument of Pentelic marble that stands where busy Leoforos Vasilissis Olgas and Leoforos Vasilissis Amalias meet. Roman emperor Hadrian erected it in AD 132, probably to commemorate the consecration of the Temple. The inscriptions show that it was also intended as a dividing point between the ancient and Roman cities. The northwest frieze reads, 'This is Athens, the Ancient city of Theseus', while the southeast frieze states, 'This is the city of Hadrian, and not of Theseus'.

☑ Top Tips

▶ Admission is included in the €12 Acropolis entry ticket.

▶ There is no shade: wear a hat and sunscreen, bring water.

▶ What you see is what you get – you can peruse the temple (and Hadrian's Arch) from outside if you're in a rush.

▶ Hours can occasionally be extended in summer. Call ahead to find out, if you'd like to visit later in the day.

✕ Take a Break

For a shady rest and a bit of nourishment, head to the verdant Zappeio Garden's Aegli Cafe (p97).

Or stroll over to Mets, a bit further afield, for a laid-back coffee at the Odeon Cafe (p96).

A B C D

1

Leof Vasilissis Amalias

👁 **4**
Roman Baths

National Gardens

Zappeio Palace

Irodou Attikou

⭐ **14**
🍴 **11**

👁 **3**

❌ **8**

Zappeio Gardens

Zappeio Gardens

Leof Vasilissis Olgas

Temple of Olympian Zeus

👁

2

Leof Vasileos Konstantinou

Plateia Stadiou

1
👁
Panathenaic Stadium

ATHANASIOU

Ardettos Hill

Ardittou

3

Theotoki

Kallirrois

Piga M

Karea

Neri K

Anapafseos

Glafkou

Miniati

Papatsoni

METS

Balanou K

🚇 **10**

Trivonianou

Stratigou Rodiou

4

Typteou

Timoleondos

Gorgiou

Harvouri

Aristonikou

Sorvolou

Fotiadou

Markou Mousourou

Arhimidous

Dikearhou

Karea

Malamou

Longinou

Stratigou Ioannou

Stratigou Domboli

Leof Vouliagmenis

Efoponou

Voulgareos Evg

⭐ **12**

Defteri

Alsos Longinou

5

Trivonianou

Iolis

Athens' First Cemetery 👁 **2**

For reviews see

👁 Top Sights	p90
⦿ Sights	p94
✕ Eating	p95
🍷 Drinking	p96
★ Entertainment	p97
🔒 Shopping	p97

Sights

Panathenaic Stadium
HISTORIC BUILDING, ANCIENT SITE

1 Map p92, D2

The grand Panathenaic Stadium, which is known as the Kalimarmaron ('beautiful marble'), was originally built in the 4th century BC for the Panathenaic athletic contests. It is said that at Hadrian's inauguration in AD 120, a thousand wild animals were sacrificed here. In AD 144 the 70,000 seats were rebuilt in Pentelic marble by Herodes Atticus. The first modern Olympic Games, in 1896, were held here and during the 2004 Olympics it made a stunning backdrop to the archery competition and marathon finish. The annual Athens marathon finishes here. (Leoforos Vasileos Konstantinou, Pangrati; adult/child €3/1.50; ⏲8am-7pm; Ⓜ Akropoli)

Athens' First Cemetery
CEMETERY

2 Map p92, C5

This resting place of many famous Greeks and philhellenes is a peaceful, quirky spot to explore. Among the cemetery's famous residents is archaeologist Heinrich Schliemann (1822–90), whose mausoleum is decorated with Trojan War scenes. Most of the tombstones and mausoleums are lavish; some have works of art created by the foremost 19th-century Greek sculptors, including Halepas' *Sleeping Maiden* on the tomb of a young girl. (Anapafseos, Trivonianou, Mets; admission free; ⏲7.30am-sunset; Ⓜ Syngrou-Fix)

Understand
Olympic History

The Olympic tradition emerged at the site of Olympia in the Peloponnese around the 11th century BC as a paean to Zeus, in the form of contests, attended initially by notable men and women who assembled before the sanctuary priests and swore to uphold solemn oaths. By the 8th century attendance had grown and the festival morphed into a male-only major event lasting five days every four years. During the competition, city-states were bound by a sacred truce to stop any fighting underway. The games ceased in AD 394 when Emperor Theodosius I banned them.

Crowds of spectators lined the tracks, where competitors vied for an honourable (and at times dishonourable) victory in athletics, chariot races, wrestling and boxing (no gloves, just simple leather straps). First prize was often a simple laurel wreath, but it was the esteem of the people that most mattered, for Greek Olympians were venerated. Three millennia later, while the scale and scope of the games may have expanded considerably, the basic format is essentially unchanged.

Panathenaic Stadium

Zappeio Gardens GARDEN

3 ⊙ Map p92, B1

These gardens are laid out in a network of wide walkways around the grand **Zappeio Palace**, built in the 1870s for the forerunner of the modern Olympics. The Zappeio hosts conferences, events and exhibitions, and has a pleasant cafe, a restaurant and an open-air cinema. (entrances on Leoforos Vasilissis Amalias & Leoforos Vasilissis Olgas, Syntagma; Ⓜ Syntagma)

Roman Baths RUINS

4 ⊙ Map p92, A1

Well-preserved ruins of a large Roman bath complex, established in the 3rd century AD, extend into the Zappeio

Gardens. (Leoforos Vasilissis Amalias; admission free; Ⓜ Syntagma)

Eating

Spondi FINE DINING €€€

5 ✕ Map p92, F4

Two Michelin-starred Spondi is consistently voted Athens' best restaurant, and the accolades are totally deserved. It offers Mediterranean haute cuisine, with heavy French influences, in a relaxed, refined setting in a charming old house. Choose off the menu or a range of set dinner and wine *prix fixes*. The restaurant has a lovely bougainvillea-draped garden. Popping the question? Come here (but book ahead, and take a cab – it's hard to reach on public transport). (📞210 752 0658; Pyrronos 5, Pangrati; mains €35-50; ⏰8pm-late)

Cucina Povera

 MEDITERRANEAN €

6 Map p92, E1

Dishes can be occasionally (but not consistently) incandescent, like the salad with avocado, pear and goat cheese. The dining room embodies relaxed hipness, and the wine list rocks. Check its website for directions. (📞210 756 6008; www.cucinapovera.gr; Efforionos 13, Pangrati; mains €9-14; ⏰dinner Tue-Sat, brunch Sun; Ⓜ Evangelismos)

Colibri

PIZZA €

7 Map p92, F4

Locals will tell you this is the best pizza in Athens. Chilled out on a quiet, tree-lined residential street with reggae wafting from inside the restaurant, order from a vast array of classic, vegetarian and gourmet pies or from a menu of pasta, burgers and salads. (📞210 701 1011; Embedokleous 9-13, Kallimarmaro, Mets; small pizzas €5.50-10, mains €5-8; 🚌2, 4, 11)

Aigli Restaurant

 MEZEDHES €€

8 Map p92, C1

Smack in the heart of the green Zappeio Gardens and next to the palace, join the crowds tucking into traditional mezedhes. These small plates range from dolmahdes to marinated anchovies. Reservations recommended. (📞210 336 9364; www.aeglizappiou.gr; Zappeio Gardens; mezedhes €5-9; ⏰dinner; Ⓜ Syntagma, Akropoli)

Vyrinis

TAVERNA €

9 Map p92, F3

Just behind the ancient Panathenaic Stadium, this popular neighbourhood taverna has had a modern makeover but maintains its essence and prices. There's a lovely courtyard garden, simple traditional fare and decent house wine. (📞210 701 2021; Arhimidous 11, Pangrati; mains €6-7; ⏰dinner Mon-Fri, lunch & dinner Sat & Sun; 🚌2, 4, 11 to Plateia Plastira)

 Local Life

Pangrati

Pangrati's **Plateia Varnava** is a great place to experience a typical Athenian neighbourhood, with families dining in the tavernas and kids playing in the square. The main shopping drag is on the streets leading up to and along **Ymittou**, which has a thriving cafe strip.

Drinking

Odeon Cafe

CAFE

10 Map p92, C4

This delightful slice of local life near corner stores and neoclassical residential buildings is a simple corner coffee shop. Quietly chatting friends sit beneath ivy winding over the sidewalk, or in the glass-fronted interior.

Occasional live music. (☎210 922 3414; Markou Mousourou 19, Mets; Ⓜ Akropoli)

Aigli Cafe
CAFE, BAR

11 Map p92, C1

This cool (literally) cafe-bar-restaurant sits among the trees in the middle of the Zappeio Gardens, with comfy loungers. It's a low-key cafe with basic food by day and at night there's mainstream music and drinks. (☎210 336 9340; Zappeio Gardens; Ⓜ Syntagma)

Entertainment

Half Note Jazz Club
JAZZ

12 Map p92, B5

Athens' stylish, principal and most serious jazz venue hosts an array of international musicians. The top line-up plays anything from classic jazz to folk and the occasional Celtic music. Book a table, or stand at the bar. (☎210 921 3310; www.halfnote.gr; Trivonianou 17, Mets; Ⓜ Akropoli)

Cafe Alavastron
LIVE MUSIC

13 Map p92, H4

It can feel like there's a band in your sitting room in this intimate, casual world-music bar, which hosts regular appearances by eclectic acts from

modern jazz to ethnic and quality Greek music. (☎210 756 0102; www.cafe alavastron.gr; Damareos 78, Pangrati)

Aigli Cinema
CINEMA

14 Map p92, C1

One of Athens' oldest and most delightful outdoor cinemas is in the middle of the gardens, ideal for a balmy night enjoying a flick with a glass of wine. (☎210 336 9369; Zappeio Gardens, Syntagma; Ⓜ Syntagma)

Shopping

Korres
COSMETICS

15 Map p92, E2

You can get the full range from this natural beauty-product guru at the company's original homeopathic pharmacy – at a fraction of the price you'll pay in London or New York. (☎210 756 0600; www.korres.com; Ivikou 8, near Panathenaic Stadium; 🚌2, 4, 11)

Bakaniko
FOOD & DRINK

16 Map p92, F4

Jam-packed local shop full of Greek products: oil, wine, cheese, nuts, honey and yogurt. Herbs hang in bunches, lentils fill sacks. (☎210 756 0055; Proklou 31, Pangrati; 🚌2, 4, 11)

Explore

National Archaeological Museum & Exarhia

Near the National Archaeological Museum, bohemian Exarhia has an alternative culture and history that sets it apart from other districts. Although partly gentrified, Exarhia retains a youthful and unconventional identity, thanks to a resident population of students, artists, actors, old lefties and intellectuals. Fantastic flights of omnipresent graffiti and occasional riot police highlight its revolutionary role.

The Sights in a Day

☀ The magnificent collections at the **National Archaeological Museum** (p100) could easily fill your whole day – wander its rooms examining priceless Greek art and artefacts. While you're there, zip alongside to the **Epigraphical Museum** (p107) for ancient inscribed tablets.

☀ Break for lunch at any of Exarhia's great restaurants, such as **Yiantes** (p107), for a rather elegant setting, or **Rozalia** (p107), for taverna-style family fare. Then take a stroll to look at the most modern of arts: fantastical and pointedly messaged graffiti.

☽ After a solid rest, plan for a late night bar-hopping Exarhia's renowned drinking holes at **Alexandrino** (p107), for classic cocktails, **Tralala** (p109), for a bohemian scene, and **Blue Fox** (p109) for retro style. Alternatively, settle in for a round of edgy live music at **An Club** (p110) and **Ginger Ale** (p110) or a late-night *rembetika* session at **Kavouras** (p110) or **Taximi** (p111).

For a local's day in Exarhia, see p104.

◉ Top Sights

National Archaeological Museum (p100)

◯ Local Life

Neighbourhood Life in Exarhia (p104)

♥ Best of Athens

Shopping

Thymari Tou Strefi (p111)

Vinyl Microstore (p105)

Metropolis Music (p111)

Entertainment

An Club (p110)

Kavouras (p110)

Taximi (p111)

Ginger Ale (p110)

Getting There

Ⓜ **Metro** Omonia station (red and green lines) is west of Exarhia. Use the Panepistimiou station (red line) for southern Exarhia.

Ⓜ **Metro** For the National Archaeological Museum, use the Viktoria station (green line).

🚎 **Trolleybus** Also for the museum, catch trolleybus 2, 4, 5, 9 or 11 from outside St Denis Cathedral (Panepistimiou 24) and get off at the Polytechnio stop.

Top Sights
National Archaeological Museum

One of the world's most important museums, the National Archaeological Museum houses the world's finest collection of Greek antiquities. Treasures offering a view of Greek art and history dating from the neolithic era to classical periods include exquisite sculptures, pottery, jewellery, frescoes and artefacts found throughout Greece. Allow plenty of time to view the vast and spectacular collections (over 11,000 displays) housed in this enormous 19th-century neoclassical building (8000 sq m). The museum also hosts world-class temporary exhibitions.

◉ Map p106, B1

www.namuseum.gr

28 Oktovriou-Patision 44, Exarhia

adult/child €7/free

⏱ 1.30-8pm Mon, 9am-4pm Tue-Sun Apr-Oct, 8.30am-3pm Nov-Mar

Ⓜ Viktoria

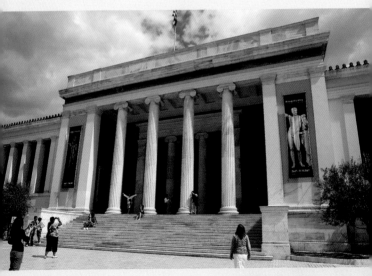

National Archaeological Museum

Don't Miss

Prehistoric Collection & Mycenaen Antiquities

Ahead of you as you enter the museum is the prehistoric collection, showcasing some of the most important pieces of Mycenaean, neolithic and Cycladic art, many in solid gold. The fabulous collection of Mycenaean antiquities (Gallery 4) is the museum's tour de force.

Mask of Agamemnon

The first cabinet holds the celebrated gold Mask of Agamemnon, unearthed at Mycenae by Heinrich Schliemann, along with key finds from Grave Circle A, including bronze daggers with intricate representations of the hunt.

Vaphio Cups

The exquisite Vaphio gold cups, with scenes of men taming wild bulls, are regarded as among the finest surviving examples of Mycenaean art. They were found in a *tholos* (Mycenaean tomb shaped like a beehive) at Vaphio, near Sparta.

Cycladic Collection

The Cycladic collection in Gallery 6 includes the superb figurines of the 3rd and 2nd millennia BC that inspired artists such as Picasso. One example measures 1.52m and dates from 2600–2300 BC.

Sounion Kouros

The galleries to the left of the entrance house the oldest and most significant pieces of the sculpture collection. Galleries 7 to 13 exhibit fine examples of Archaic *kouroi* (male statues) from the 7th century BC to 480 BC. The colossal 600 BC Sounion Kouros (Room 8), found at the Temple of Poseidon in Sounion, is made of Naxian marble and stood before Poseidon's temple.

PANORAMIC IMAGES/GETTY IMAGES ©

☑ **Top Tips**

▶ Arrive early in the day or late in the evening to beat the rush.

▶ Allow plenty of time: with 8000 sq m of exhibition space, it could take several visits to appreciate the museum's vast holdings, but it's possible to see the highlights in a half-day.

▶ Exhibits are displayed largely thematically. For more information get an audioguide.

✕ **Take a Break**

The **museum cafe** in the basement extends into an open-air internal courtyard. Or nip outside for coffee at **La Favorita** (Tositsa 8, Exarhia; Ⓜ Viktoria), an airy cafe around the corner.

For a meal, the best bet is to head into Exarhia, to a place like Yiantes (p107) for fresh modern Greek food with a glass of wine.

National Archaeological Museum

First Floor

Cypriot Collection
Pottery Collection
Pottery Collection
Panathenaic Amphorae
Lift
Thira Gallery
Minoan Frescoes from Santorini

Ground Floor

Stathatos Collection
Egyptian Collection
Lift
Statue of Horse & Young Rider
Aphrodite
Statue of Zeus
Vaphio Cups
Lift
Athena Varvakeion
Prehistoric Collection
Mycenaen Antiquities
Mask of Agamemnon
Cycladic Collection
Sounion Kouros
Entrance

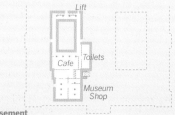

Basement

Lift
Toilets
Cafe
Museum Shop

Bronze God

Gallery 15 is dominated by the incredible 460-BC bronze statue of Zeus or Poseidon, found in the sea off Evia, which depicts one of the gods (no one really knows which) with his arms outstretched and holding a thunderbolt or trident in his right hand.

Athena Varvakeion

The 200-BC statue of Athena Varvakeion in Gallery 20 is the most famous copy – much reduced in size – of the colossal statue of Athena Polias by Pheidias that once stood in the Parthenon.

Horse & Rider

In Gallery 21 you will see the striking 2nd-century-BC statue of a horse and young rider, recovered from a shipwreck off Cape Artemision in Evia. Opposite the horse are several lesser-known but equally exquisite works such as the statue of Aphrodite, showing a demure nude Aphrodite struggling to hold her draped gown over herself.

Egyptian Gallery

The two-room (40 and 41) Egyptian gallery presents the best of the museum's significant collection, the only one in Greece. Dating from 5000 BC to the Roman conquest, artefacts include mummies, Fayum portraits and bronze figurines.

Stathatos Collection

The Stathatos private collection (gallery 42) is a precious array of small pieces from the middle Bronze Age to the Byzantine period and beyond.

Minoan Frescoes

Upstairs, the spectacular Minoan frescoes from Santorini (Thira) were uncovered in the prehistoric settlement of Akrotiri, which was buried by a volcanic eruption in the late 16th century BC. The frescoes include *Boxing Children* and *Spring,* depicting red lilies and a pair of swallows kissing in midair. The Thira Gallery also has videos showing the 1926 eruption and the Akrotiri excavation.

Pottery Collection

The superb pottery collection traces the development of pottery from the Bronze Age through the Protogeometric and Geometric periods, to the famous Attic black-figured pottery (6th century BC), and red-figured pottery (late 5th to early 4th centuries BC). Other uniquely Athenian vessels are the Attic White Lekythoi, slender vases depicting scenes at tombs.

Panathenaic Amphorae

In the centre of Gallery 56 are six Panathenaic amphorae, presented to the winners of the Panathenaic Games. Each amphora (vase-shaped ceramic vessel) contained oil from the sacred olive trees of Athens and victors might have received up to 140 of them. They are painted with scenes from the relevant sport (in this case wrestling) on one side and an armed Athena Promachos on the other.

Local Life
Neighbourhood Life in Exarhia

Exarhia has an eclectic mix of comic stores, record shops, publishing houses and alternative book and clothing stores. It has a vibrant bar scene, particularly the crowded student hang-outs on Mesolongiou, good-value eateries, and rock and *rembetika* (Greek blues) clubs. Plateia Exarhion (Exarhion Sq) is the local focal point, with many tavernas along pedestrian Valtestiou and Benaki, and bustling cafes and bars around nearly every corner.

❶ Plateia Exarhion
Plateia Exarhion is the epicentre of neighbourhood life. Pick a spot on the square for prime people-watching. Locals choose modern cafe-bookshop **Floral** (Themistokleous 80, Exarhia; 🛜; Ⓜ Omonia), with grey-toned images of retro life and, you guessed it, flowers on the walls. Folks buy books, use the wi-fi, chat and watch the world go by. It's a good place to start the day or evening before exploring.

2 Graffiti A-Go-Go

The walls, alleys and stairways of Exarhia are adorned with, possibly, some of the world's most creative graffiti. Often with a pointed underlying political message, these elaborate works are an inspiration to behold. Start at the Strefi Hill end of Themistokleous and simply wander the neighbourhood, looking for the latest expressions of both fancy and ire.

3 Reclaimed Square

The inhabitants of Exarhia took back an entire city block, turning it into a completely locally planted and maintained urban park. See the reclaimed square bordered by Didetou, Harilaou Trikoupi, Navarinou and Zoodohou Pigis – a real work in progress.

4 Old-World Taverna

Lunch at Exarhia institution **Barbagiannis** (210 330 0185; Emmanuel Benaki 94, Exarhia; mains €5-7; lunch & dinner Mon-Sat, to 7pm Sun; Omonia), an extremely low-key *mayirio* (cook house) on a quiet corner. Choose from the variety of big trays of traditional dishes behind the counter, such as *pastitsio* (layers of baked macaroni and minced meat), washed down with house wine.

5 Boho Lunch

Or slip over to **Kimatothrafstis** (213 030 8274; Harilaou Trikoupi 49, Exarhia; small/large plate €3.80/6.80; 8am-11pm, closed dinner Sun; Omonia), a great-value, bright and casual modern cafe with communal tables. Choose from the buffet of the day's offerings: a range of home-style Greek cooking and alternative fare. Plates come in two sizes: big or small.

6 Record Shopping

Exarhia's fun music shops include the chance to pick up, among other things, old-school vinyl. Serious music fans comb **Vinyl Microstore** (210 361 4544; www.vmradio.gr; Didotou 34, Exarhia; Panepistimio) for eclectic indie, alternative and dance vinyl releases and CDs over a coffee. The owners organise party tours, art exhibitions in the basement and an indie music festival. **Spindle** (www.spindlevinylrecords. gr; 49 Didotou, Exarhia; Panepistimio) is across the street.

7 Go Cretan for Dinner

Neighbourhood denizens love **Oxo Nou** (210 380 1778; Emmanuel Benaki 63-65, cnr Metaxa, Exarhia; mains €8-11; 3pm-late daily; Omonia) for its super Cretan food. This cheery new restaurant with large plate glass windows serves a widely praised range of the island's specialities.

8 Live Local Music

Athenians come to Exarhia for its off-beat bars, live-music venues and *rembetika* clubs. See our listings for a complete array of choices, or hop down to the bar strip at **Mesolongiou** to start your night, and see what happens.

Sights

Epigraphical Museum
MUSEUM

1 Map p106, B2

This 'library of stones' houses an important collection of Greek inscriptions detailing official records, including lists of war dead, tribute lists showing annual payments by Athens' allies, and the decree ordering the evacuation of Athens before the 480 BC Persian invasion. (📞210 821 7637; www.culture.gr; Tositsa 1, Exarhia; ⏱8.30am-3pm Tue-Sun; Ⓜ Viktoria)

Eating

Yiantes
TAVERNA €€

2 Map p106, C3

This modern eatery with its white linen and freshcut flowers set in a garden courtyard is upmarket for Exarhia, but the food is superb and made with largely organic produce. Try interesting greens such as *almirikia*, the perfectly grilled fish, delicious mussels, or risotto with mushrooms and truffle oil. It occasionally offers a fixed three-course menu (€13.50) with wine. (📞210 330 1369; Valtetsiou 44, Exarhia; mains €9-10; Ⓜ Omonia)

Rozalia
TAVERNA €

3 Map p106, C3

An old-style Exarhia favourite on a lively pedestrian strip, this family-run taverna serves grills and home-style fare such as *pastitsio* (layers of buttery macaroni and seasoned minced lamb). Large courtyard/garden fans spray water to keep you cool, and on Sunday it's packed with families. (📞210 330 2933; Valtetsiou 58, Exarhia; mains €5-11; Ⓜ Omonia)

Byzantino tou Strefi
MEZEDHES €

4 Map p106, E2

Escape up Strefi Hill to this casual *mezedhopoleio*, where you can enjoy good-value mezedhes in a peaceful setting away from the urban jungle. (📞694 737 8285; enter from steps near Emmanuel Benaki 126; mezedhes €3-8; ⏱6pm-late Mon-Fri, noon-late Sat & Sun; Ⓜ Omonia)

Drinking

Alexandrino
BAR

5 Map p106, C3

There's a quaint French-bistro feel to this tiny bar on the emerging dining and bar strip along Benaki. Alexandrino is great for a quiet drink with excellent wines and cocktails. The service is friendly and you can sit at

☑ Top Tip

Safety
While Exarhia is a mainstay residential neighbourhood, it has been known to be sketchy (petty thefts) at night. During times of political protest it is best to steer clear. Keep informed and use your common sense.

Understand

Greece's Military Dictatorship

Exarhia's anarchic reputation has roots in its association with radical politics and the infamous student sit-in at the neighbourhood's **Athens Polytechnio** (Technical University), under the junta. This military dictatorship was headed by a group of army colonels, led by Georgios Papadopoulos and Stylianos Patakos, who staged a coup on 21 April 1967. They established a military junta with Papadopoulos as prime minister. King Constantine attempted a counter-coup in December before fleeing the country.

Total Domination

The colonels declared martial law, banned political parties and trade unions, imposed censorship and imprisoned, tortured and exiled thousands of dissidents, including actress and activist Melina Mercouri. In June 1972 Papadopoulos declared Greece a republic and appointed himself president. On 17 November 1973 tanks stormed a building at the Athens Polytechnio to quell a student occupation calling for an uprising against the US-backed junta. While the number of casualties is still in dispute, the act spelt the death knell for the junta.

The Fall of the Junta

Shortly after, the head of the military security police, Dimitrios Ioannidis, deposed Papadopoulos. In July 1974 Ioannidis tried to impose unity with Cyprus by attempting to topple the Makarios government in Cyprus; Makarios got wind of an assassination attempt and escaped. The junta replaced him with the extremist Nikos Sampson (a former right-wing Greek Cypriot National Organisation of Cypriot Freedom Fighters (EOKA) leader) as president. Consequently, Turkey occupied northern Cyprus, partitioning the country and displacing almost 200,000 Greek Cypriots who fled their homes for the safety of the south. The junta dictatorship collapsed.

Restoration of Democracy

Konstandinos Karamanlis was summoned from Paris to take office and his New Democracy (ND) party won a large majority in elections held in 1974 against the newly formed Panhellenic Socialist Union (PASOK), led by Andreas Papandreou (son of Georgios). A plebiscite voted 69% against the restoration of the monarchy and a ban on communist parties was lifted.

Alexandrino (p107)

the narrow bar or at the few tables on the pavement. (Emmanuel Benaki 69, Exarhia; Omonia)

Tralala
BAR

6 Map p106, D4

This arty hang-out on the outskirts of Exarhia, popular with actors, does a roaring coffee trade by day, while in the evening the cool crowd spills out onto the pavement. Original artwork, lively owners and gregarious atmosphere. (Asklipiou 45, Exarhia; Panepistimio)

Vox
BAR

7 Map p106, C3

Vox is a good place to start on the square – linger over coffee during the

day, or join the crowd of liquoring locals at night. Live Greek music fills the joint on some weekends. (Themistokleous 80, Exarhia; Omonia)

Blue Fox
BAR

8 Map p106, E3

You might not expect this in Athens, but Blue Fox is great for '50s-era swing and rockabilly complete with Vespas and poodle skirts. (Asklipiou 91, Exarhia; Omonia)

Circus
BAR

9 Map p106, C4

Right on the border of Kolonaki and Exarhia, Circus has Exarhia's youthful edge without the grunge and a bit of Kolonaki's glamour without the pretensions. Presided over by a Ganesh-style wire elephant, Circus has relaxed coffees by day and cocktails by night. (www.circusbar.gr; Navarinou 11, Exarhia; **M**Panepistimiou)

Entertainment

Ginger Ale
LIVE MUSIC, BAR

10 ⭐ Map p106, C3

Dip back in time to a '50s veneered coffee shop–cum–rocking nightspot. Sip espresso by day and catch a rotating line-up of live acts by night. (🖉 210 330 1246; http://ginger-ale.gr; Themistokleous 80, Exarhia; **M**Omonia)

An Club
LIVE MUSIC

11 ⭐ Map p106, B3

Exarhia's popular basement rock club hosts lesser-known international bands, as well as some interesting local acts. (🖉 210 330 5056; www.anclub.gr; Solomou 13-15, Exarhia; **M**Omonia)

Kavouras
REMBETIKA

12 ⭐ Map p106, C3

Above Exarhia's all-night souvlaki joint, this lively club has a decent line-up of musicians playing *rembetika* until dawn for a student crowd. No cover charge after 1am. (🖉 210 381 0202; Themistokleous 64, Exarhia; ⏱11pm-late Thu-Sat, closed Jul & Aug; **M**Omonia)

Understand
Greek Music Scene

Athens has a thriving live-music scene in winter, when you can hear the gamut of Greek music, from the popular soulful Greek blues known as *rembetika* to traditional folk music, ethnic jazz, and even Greek rock, rap and hip hop. Athens' many intimate winter venues (most only operate between October and April) also host an eclectic range of touring indie rock, jazz and international artists. In summer, live music is confined to festivals and outdoor concerts by local artists and touring acts.

The mainstays of Athenian nightlife are the *bouzoukia*, glitzy and expensive cabaret-style venues (often referred to as *skyladika* – dog houses – because of the crooning singers), where women dancing the sinewy *tsifteteli* (belly dance) are showered with expensive trays of carnations and revellers party until sunrise.

Popular Greek artists include consummate mainstream performers such as Haris Alexiou, Eleftheria Arvanitaki, George Dalaras, Dimitra Galani and Alkistis Protopsalti. Greece's big pop acts put on spectacular shows – look out for Anna Vissi, Antonis Remos, Despina Vandi, Notis Sfakianakis, Ploutarhos, Sakis Rouvas, Mihalis Hatziyiannis and Elena Paparizou.

Taximi
REMBETIKA

13 ⭐ Map p106, E3

Most of Greece's major *rembetika* players have performed here since it opened 20 years ago. It has gone a little upmarket – and expensive – but is still popular for authentic *rembetika*. Go weeknights for more elbow room. (☎210 363 9919; Isavron 29, cnr Harilaou Trikoupi, Exarhia; ⏱11pm-late Tue-Sat; Ⓜ Panepistimio)

Shopping

Thymari Tou Strefi
FOOD & WINE

14 🔒 Map p106, D2

Right in the thick of Saturday's lively street market, this quaint deli has a delectable array of traditional products, honey, cheese and regional specialities, as well as organic wine and ouzo. (☎210 330 0384; Kalidromiou 51A, Exarhia; ⏱9am-6pm Mon & Wed, to 9pm Tue, Thu & Fri, 8am-4pm Sat ; Ⓜ Omonia)

Ⓠ Local Life
Saturday Steet Market

Every Saturday morning locals make the trek up to the Kalidromiou, in the foothills of Strefi Hill, to Exarhia's weekly **farmer's market** (⏱6am-2pm; 🚌026, Ⓜ Omonia) or *laïki agora*, an enduring Athens institution. One of Athens' most atmospheric markets sees rowdy traders hawk fresh produce and household goods over one of Exarhia's finest streets. Get a prime seat at one of the busy cafes.

Metropolis Music
MUSIC

15 🔒 Map p106, A4

This major music store is well stocked with Greek and international CDs and sells concert tickets. (☎210 383 0804; Panepistimiou 64, Omonia; Ⓜ Omonia)

Explore

Filopappou Hill & Thisio

Filopappou Hill, also known as the Hill of the Muses, offers the best eye-level views of the Acropolis. The sedate Thisio neighbourhood, just to the north, blossomed after cars were banished to make way for the pedestrian promenade. Young Athenians have claimed the cafe precinct that emerged under the Acropolis and the low-key residential streets make a nice change from the more heavily touristed centre.

The Sights in a Day

Stroll **Filopappou Hill** (p114) in the morning, photographing the Acropolis, the Saronic Gulf and the mountains of the Attic basin. On its slopes explore ancient battlements, a shrine to the muses, Socrates' prison and a quiet Byzantine church.

Then lunch in Thisio on traditional Greek fare at **Gevomai Kai Magevomai** (p119) or **Filistron** (p119) and relax with a long coffee-drinking and people-watching session, as the locals do, on the cafe strips. Or, stop in at **Peonia Herbs** (p120) for a special tea experience. When you're rejuvinated, take in a bit of modern art: **Herakleidon Museum** (p117) has work by Escher and Vasarely, while **Bernier-Eliades** (p117) shows high-profile contemporary art.

Get tickets for **Dora Stratou Dance Theatre** (p121) to see an amazing array of Greek dances in elaborate costumes in an open-air theatre on Filopappou Hill, or watch a movie at the equally alfresco **Thission** (p121) – which has Acropolis views – then hit the bars.

⊙ Top Sights

Filopappou Hill (p114)

♥ Best of Athens

Food

Filistron (p119)

Gevomai Kai Magevomai (p119)

Entertainment

Dora Stratou Dance Theatre (p121)

Thission (p121)

Getting There

Ⓜ **Metro** To enter the Thisio neighbourhood directly, use the Thisio station (green line) and walk up pedestrianised Apostolou Pavlou.

Ⓜ **Metro** To reach Filopappou Hill, either walk through Thisio, or use the Akropoli station (red line) and walk west, by the Acropolis Museum on either Rovertou Galli or pedestrianised Dionysiou Areopagitou.

Top Sights
Filopappou Hill

Also called the Hill of the Muses, Filopappou Hill – along with the Hills of the Pnyx and Nymphs – was, according to Plutarch, where Thesues and the Amazons did battle. Inhabited from prehistoric times to the post-Byzantine era, today the pine-clad slopes are a relaxing place for a stroll. They offer excellent views of Attica and the Saronic Gulf, and some of the very best vantage points for photographing the Acropolis. There are also some notable ruins.

⊙ Map p116, C5

Ⓜ Akropoli

Filopappou Hill

Don't Miss

Church of Agios Dimitrios Loumbardiaris
The 16th-century **Church of Agios Dimitrios Loumbardiaris** (Greek for cannon) is named after an incident in which a gunner from a Turkish garrison on the Acropolis was killed by a thunderbolt while attempting to fire a cannon on the Christian congregation. It has an old-world feel with a smell of incense, marble floors, a timber roof, and myriad icons and frescoes.

Socrates' Prison
Enter the cover of pines, with doves cooing, and follow the path to this warren of rooms carved into bedrock and rumoured to have been the place Socrates was **imprisoned**. During WWII artefacts from the Acropolis and National Archaeological Museum were secreted here, sealed behind a wall.

Shrine of the Muses
Follow the stairs up the hill, and you'll reach a ruined shrine to the **Muses**, to whom this hill was deemed sacred. Even today grateful or hopeful artists place offerings on a small stone cairn.

Fortifications
According to myth, this hill was a strategic bastion for Athenians defending against Amazons. In the 4th and 5th centuries BC, defensive walls – such as the Themistoclean wall and the Diateichisma – stretched over the hill. Extensive ruins still remain.

Monument of Filopappos
The 12m **Monument of Filopappos** crowns the summit of the hill. Built between Ad 114 and 116 in honour of Julius Antiochus Filopappos, a Roman consul and administrator, the top middle niche depicted Filopappos enthroned, the bottom frieze showed him in a chariot with his entourage.

☑ **Top Tips**

▶ Small paths weave all over the hill, but the paved path to the top starts near the *periptero* (kiosk) on Dionysiou Areopagitou.

▶ Bring camera gear: the summit gives one of the best views of the Acropolis and Attica – sunset and evening offer spectacular light.

▶ Above the treeline the hill is exposed: bring sunscreen, a hat and water; rain gear on wet days.

▶ Informative English-language placards placed at major features explain the rich ancient history of the hill.

✗ **Take a Break**

For refreshment, drop down to the cafes in Thisio, or restaurants such as Filistron (p119) and Gevomai Kai Magevomai (p119).

Alternatively, just at the hill's base (as you head back towards the Acropolis Museum), lovely Dionysos (p35) offers drinks with views or a fine meal.

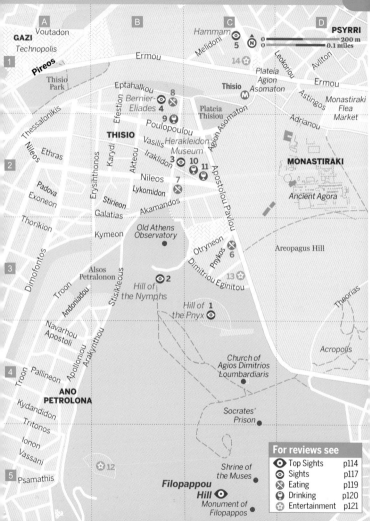

GAZI

Voutadon

Technopolis

Pireos

Hammam

Melidoni

5

PSYRRI

Leokoriou

Aviliton

Ermou

Ermou

14

Plateia
Agion
Asomaton

Astingos

Adrianou

Monastiraki
Flea
Market

Thisio
Park

Thessalonikis

Nileos

Ethras

Padova

Exoneon

Thorikion

Dimofontos

Troon

Eptahalkou

Bernier-
Eliades

Efestion

8

4

9

Poulopoulou

THISIO

Karydi

Akteou

Vasilis

Iraklidon

Herakleidon
Museum

3

10

11

Nileos

Lykomidon

7

Stirieon

Galatias

Akamandos

Thisio

M

Plateia
Thisiou

Agion Asomaton

Apostolou Pavlou

MONASTIRAKI

Ancient Agora

Erysithonos

Kymeon

Old Athens
Observatory

Otryneon

6

Pnykos

13

Areopagus Hill

Alsos
Petralonon

Andoniadou

Stisikleous

2

Hill of
the Nymphs

Dimitriou Eginitou

Theorias

Navarhou
Apostoli

Apolloniou

Arakynthou

Hill of
the Pnyx

1

Acropolis

Troon

Pallineon

ANO
PETROLONA

Church of
Agios Dimitrios
Loumbardiaris

Kydandidon

Tritonos

Ionon

Vassani

Socrates'
Prison

Psamathis

12

Shrine of
the Muses

Filopappou
Hill

Monument of
Filopappos

200 m

0.1 miles

For reviews see	
◉ Top Sights	p114
◉ Sights	p117
✕ Eating	p119
🍷 Drinking	p120
☆ Entertainment	p121

Sights

Hill of the Pnyx   LANDMARK, PARK

1  Map p116, C3

North of Filopappou, this rocky hill was the meeting place of the Democratic Assembly in the 5th century BC, where the great orators Aristides, Demosthenes, Pericles and Themistocles addressed assemblies. This less-visited site offers great views over Athens and a peaceful walk. At the Thisio base of the hill, along Apostolou Pavlou, find the **Kallirroe Fountain** next to the **Sanctuary of Pan**. (**M**Thisio)

Hill of the Nymphs   LANDMARK, PARK

2 Map p116, B3

Northwest of Hill of the Pnyx, this hill is home to the **old Athens observatory**, built in 1842. (**M**Thisio)

Herakleidon Museum   ART MUSEUM

3 Map p116, B2

This superb private museum showcases how art, mathematics and philosophy interrelate. The permanent collection includes one of the world's biggest collections of MC Escher, as well as Victor Vasarely, all in a beautifully restored neoclassical mansion. Extensive educational progams include excellent two-hour guided-tour seminars in English, available with advance booking (€25, minimum of 10 participants required). (210 346 1981; www.herakleidon-art.gr; Herakleidon 16, Thisio; adult/child €6/free; 1-9pm Fri, 11am-7pm Sat & Sun; **M**Thisio)

GEORGE TSAFOS/GETTY IMAGES ©

Herakleidon Museum

Bernier-Eliades   GALLERY

4 Map p116, B1

This well-established gallery showcases prominent Greek artists and an impressive list of international artists, from abstract American impressionists to British pop. (210 341 3935; www.bernier-eliades.gr; Eptachalkou 11, Thisio; 10.30am-8pm Tue-Fri, noon 4pm Sat; **M**Thisio)

Hammam   SPA

5 Map p116, C1

This new little spa combines classics such as marble basins with modern amenities. It offers the full range of services from a basic *hammam* (€25) to a host of massages and treatments. (210 323 1073; www.hammam.gr; Agion

Understand

Greek Gods

Ancient Greece revolved around a worship of 12 central gods and god-desses, all of which played a major role in the *mythos* (mythology). Each city-state had its own patron god or goddess, to be appeased and flattered, while on a personal level a farmer might make sacrifice to the goddess Demeter to bless his crops, or a fisherman to Poseidon to bring him fish and safe passage on the waves.

The Ancient Pantheon

▶ **Zeus (Jupiter)** Heavyweight champ of Mt Olympus, lord of the skies and master of disguise in pursuit of mortal maidens.

▶ **Poseidon (Neptune)** God of the seas, master of the mists and younger brother of Zeus.

▶ **Hera (Juno)** Protector of women and family, the queen of heaven was also the embattled wife of Zeus.

▶ **Hades (Pluto)** God of death, he ruled the underworld, bringing in newly dead with the help of his skeletal ferryman, Charon.

▶ **Athena (Minerva)** Goddess of wisdom, war and science, and guardian of Athens.

▶ **Aphrodite (Venus)** Goddess of love and beauty.

▶ **Apollo** God of music, light, the arts and fortune-telling.

▶ **Artemis (Diana)** The goddess of the hunt and twin sister of Apollo was, ironically, patron saint of wild animals.

▶ **Ares (Mars)** God of war. Zeus' least favourite of his progeny.

▶ **Hermes (Mercury)** Messenger of the gods, patron saint of travellers.

▶ **Hephaestus (Vulcan)** God of craftsmanship, metallurgy and fire; he made the world's first woman of clay, Pandora, as a punishment for man.

▶ **Hestia (Vesta)** Goddess of the hearth, in the public domain she pro-tected the city's sacred central hearth.

Asomaton 17 & Melidoni 1, Thisio; 🕙 1-10pm Tue-Fri, 10am-10pm Sat & Sun; Ⓜ Thisio)

Eating

Filistron MEZEDHES €€

6 Map p116, C3

It's wise to book a prized table on the rooftop terrace of this excellent *mezedhopoleio*, which enjoys breath-taking Acropolis and Lykavittos views. Specialising in regional cuisine, it has a great range of tasty mezedhes – try the grilled vegetables with haloumi or the Mytiline onions stuffed with rice and mince – and an extensive Greek wine list. (🖉 210 346 7554; Apostolou Pavlou 23, Thisio; mezedhes €8-14; 🕙 lunch & dinner Tue-Sun; Ⓜ Thisio)

Gevomai Kai Magevomai TAVERNA €

7 Map p116, B2

Stroll off the pedestrian way to find this small corner taverna with marble-topped tables. Neighbouring locals know it as one of the best for home-cooked, simple food with the freshest ingredients. (🖉 210 345 2802; www.gevome-magevome.gr; Nileos 11, Thisio; mains €6-9; 🕙 lunch & dinner Tue-Sun; 🛜 ; Ⓜ Thisio)

To Steki tou Ilia TAVERNA €

8 Map p116, B1

You'll often see people waiting for a table at this *psistaria* (restaurant serving grilled food), famous for its tasty grilled lamb and pork chops, sold by the kilo. With tables under the trees

---

Understand

Early Greek Philosophers

- -

Late 5th- and early-4th-century-BC philosophers Aristotle, Plato and Socrates introduced new ways of thinking rooted not in the mysticism of myths, but rather in rationality, with a focus on logic and reason. Athens' greatest citizen, Socrates (469-399 BC), was forced to drink hemlock for his disbelief in the old gods, but before he died he bequethed a school of hypothetical reductionism that is still used today. Plato (427–347 BC), his star student, was responsible for documenting his teacher's thoughts for posterity. Considered an idealist, he wrote *The Republic* as a warning to the city-state of Athens that unless its people respected law, leadership and educated its youth sufficiently, it would be doomed. His student Aristotle (384–322 BC), at the end of the Golden Age, was the personal physician to Philip II, King of Macedon, and the tutor of Alexander the Great, and focused his gifts on astronomy, physics, zoology, ethics and politics. The greatest gift of the Athenian philosophers to modern-day thought is their spirit of rational inquiry.

Street dining at Stavlos

on the quiet pedestrian strip opposite the church, it's a no-frills place with barrel wine and simple dips, chips and salads. (📞210 345 8052; Eptahalkou 5, Thisio; chops per portion/kg €9/30; ⏰8pm-late; Ⓜ Thisio)

Top Tip

Drinking in Thisio

Cafes along Thisio's pedestrian promenade **Apostolou Pavlou** have great Acropolis views. The string of cafes and bars along pedestrianised **Iraklidon** also draws 'em in. So just wander and see what appeals.

Drinking

Peonia Herbs

TEA HOUSE

9 🕹 Map p116, B2

There's an instantly calming, smoke-free aura to this herb shop and tearoom, where you can sip on a range of exotic teas while staff rustle up local herbal remedies in the workshop on the mezzanine. (📞210 341 0260; Amfiktionos 12, Thisio; ⏰10am-4pm Mon-Fri, to 3pm Sat; Ⓜ Thisio)

Stavlos

CAFE, BAR

10 🕹 Map p116, C2

Located in the old royal stables, this is one of the original bars in the thriving

Thisio strip. There's a great internal courtyard bar, as well as tables on the pavement outside, some with Acropolis views. At night it gets thumping with a disco beat and a youngish crowd. (Iraklidon 10, Thisio; M Thisio)

Sin Athina
CAFE, BAR

11 Map p116, C2

Location, location, location! This little cafe-bar sits just at the junction of the two pedestrianised cafe strips, and has a sweeping view up to the Acropolis. The outside tables are cooled with water-fans in summer. (210 345 5550; www.sinathina.gr; Iraklidon 2, Thisio; M Thisio)

Entertainment

Dora Stratou Dance Theatre
TRADITIONAL DANCE

12 Map p116, B5

Every summer since 1965, this company has performed its repertoire of Greek folk dances at its open-air theatre on the western side of Filopappou Hill. Formed to preserve the country's folk culture, it has gained an international reputation and some of its costumes are museum pieces. It also runs folk-dancing workshops in summer. The theatre is signposted from the western end of Dionysiou Areopagitou; the daytime box office is

at Scholiou 8, in Plaka. (210 921 4650; www.grdance.org; Filopappou Hill; adult/child €15/5; ⏰performances 9.30pm Wed-Fri, 8.15pm Sat & Sun Jun-Sep, closed 15-19 Aug; M Petralona)

Thission
CINEMA

13 Map p116, C3

Across from the Acropolis, this is a lovely old-style cinema in a garden setting. Sit towards the back if you want to catch a glimpse of the glowing edifice. (210 342 0864; Apostolou Pavlou 7, Thisio; M Thisio)

Loop
CLUB, LIVE MUSIC

14 Map p116, C1

Folks gather in a semi-industrial area to rock out to top DJs and occasional live acts. (210 324 7666; Plateia Agion Asomaton 3, Thisio; M Thisio)

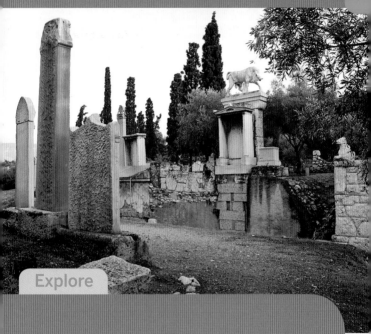

Explore

Keramikos & Gazi

Like a beacon, the illuminated red chimneys of the old Athens gas-works (Technopolis) lead you to Gazi, the city's best nightlife district. Cool restaurants, bars and nightclubs alternate with museums, theatres and art spaces. If you go by foot from Thisio via pedestrianised Ermou you pass Keramikos, the archaeological site of the city's ancient cemetery and home of another excellent museum.

The Sights in a Day

Begin at **Keramikos** (p124) and explore the extensive grounds and elaborate monuments early in the day – before it gets too hot. Then pop into its museum for superior sculptural artefacts. The nearby **Museum of Islamic Art** (p129) is a fine showcase of an extensive, exquisite collection and is certainly worth a visit.

Take a break for lunch in Gazi at any number of fine eateries, such as **Kanella** (p130), a trendy taverna with tasty basics. Then head down to the modern art museum, **Benaki Museum Pireos Annexe** (p129) for top exhibitions, finishing with a coffee in its spacious cafe.

Be sure to take a long nap so you can be out all night. For dinner, you can cab it to high-end **Varoulko** (p130) for sublime seafood or down-home **Skoufias** (p130) for classic regional cuisine. Or take the metro directly to Gazi for one of the tavernas near the square, or **Jamon** (p131) for a tapas warm-up. When you're ready, the bar crawl begins...start at **Hoxton** (p131) and see what happens.

For a local's night out in Gazi, see p126.

Top Sights

Keramikos (p124)

Local Life

A Night Out in Gazi (p126)

Best of Athens

Museums

Museum of Islamic Art (p129)

Benaki Museum Pireos Annex (p129)

Food

Kanella (p130)

Skoufias (p130)

Varoulko (p130)

Getting There

M Metro The Keramikos station (blue line) pops up in the centre of the Gazi neighbourhood. Parking is atrocious, so certainly use the metro.

M Metro To reach the Keramikos archaeological site the Thisio station (green line) is a hair closer... just walk up Ermou to the site entrance.

Top Sights
Keramikos

A cemetery from 3000 BC to the 6th century AD (Roman times), Keramikos was originally a settlement for potters who were attracted by the clay on the banks of the River Iridanos. Because of frequent flooding, the area was ultimately converted to being the city's primary cemetery, and now lies below street level due to the silt deposits. Rediscovered by a worker in 1861 during the construction of Pireos street, Keramikos is now a lush, tranquil site with a fine museum and a collection of magnificent sculptures.

◉ Map p128, D2

☎ 210 346 3552

Ermou 148, Keramikos

adult/child incl museum €2/free, free with Acropolis pass

⊙ 8am-8pm Apr-Oct, 8.30am-3pm Nov-Mar

Ⓜ Thisio

Keramikos

Don't Miss

The Grounds

Once inside you'll find a plan of the site. A path leads down to the right to the remains of the city wall built by Themistocles in 479 BC, and rebuilt by Konon in 394 BC and around the grounds. The wall is broken by the foundations of two gates; tiny signs mark each one.

Sacred Gate

The Sacred Gate spanned the **Sacred Way**, along which pilgrims from Eleusis entered the city during the annual **Eleusian procession**. Between the Sacred and Dipylon Gates are the foundations of the **Pompeion**, used as an important ceremonial centre for the **Panathenaic Procession** (p43).

Dipylon Gate

The once-massive Dipylon Gate was the city's main entrance and where the Panathenaic Procession began. It was also where the city's prostitutes gathered to offer their services to travellers. From a platform nearby, Pericles gave his famous speech extolling the virtues of Athens.

Street of Tombs

This avenue was reserved for the tombs of Athens' most prominent citizens. Some surviving *stelae* (grave slabs) are now in the on-site museum and the National Archaeological Museum; what you see are mostly replicas.

Archaeological Museum of Keramikos

The small but excellent museum contains remarkable *stelae* and sculptures from the site, such as the amazing 4th-century-BC **marble bull** from the plot of Dionysos of Kollytos, as well as funerary offerings and ancient toys.

☑ Top Tips

▶ Do not skip the museum – it contains superb original sculptures (reproductions were placed among the tombs when the sculptures were moved indoors for their protection)

▶ Bring your imagination: though many of the ceremonial buildings and gates no longer exist, this was a monumental gateway to the city for the ancients.

▶ Also bring water as there is no cafe or shop really nearby.

▶ Admission to the site and the museum is included in the Acropolis ticket.

✕ Take a Break

Either head to the cafes in Gazi for a sandwich or drink, or return towards the city centre on Ermou to the Thisio and Monastiraki neighbourhoods.

Local Life
A Night Out in Gazi

The warren of streets in Gazi emanating away from its central *plateia* are chock-a-block with thriving restaurants and bars. The hottest nightlife district in the city, it exploded in popularity after the city's former gasworks were turned into the Technopolis cultural centre. The towering pylons are illuminated red at night, calling all partygoers.

❶ Dinner on the Square

Decked out in cool mod fittings, Gazi trailblazer **Mamacas** (☎210 346 4984; http://mamacas.gr; Persefonis 41, Gazi; mains €12-19; Ⓜ Keramikos) kicked off the 'modern taverna' trend, serving home-style food in a bold white-on-white setting. It has since expanded across the road and added a club. The tables stretching across the front terraces provide the perfect vantage point for sizing up the action ringing the entire *plateia*.

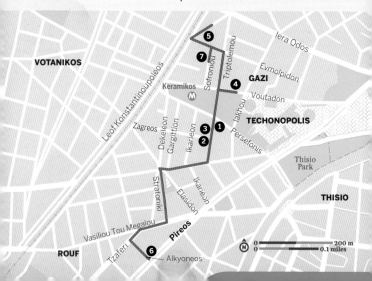

❷ Go Greek

Another summer favourite is **Dirty Ginger** (📞 210 342 3809; www.dirtyginger. gr; Triptolemou 46, Gazi; 🕐 dinner May-Oct; Ⓜ Keramikos), with tables around a giant palm tree in the colourfully lit courtyard. It specialises in meat dishes, and the place progressively morphs into a noisy, lively bar as the night wears on.

❸ Tapas to Start

To lay a lighter base for the night ahead, go to **Tapas** (Triptolemou 44, Gazi; Ⓜ Keramikos) to sup on a yummy array of small tapa plates while you sip delish cocktails to soothing beats. You can sit streetside and watch the crowds cascade into the neighbour-hood, or hop up to the balcony for panoramic views.

❹ Heating it Up, With a View

In summer, don't judge the action at ground level, head to the rooftop terraces. You'll find one of the best at **Gazarte** (📞 210 346 0347; www.gazarte. gr; Voutadon 32-34, Gazi; Ⓜ Keramikos), where a cinema-sized video screen is dwarfed by the amazing city views taking in the Acropolis. Mainstream music and occasional live acts please a trendy 30-something crowd. There's also a cinema proper and a restaurant to boot.

❺ Gay Gazi

Gazi has quietly come to have one of Athens' best gay and lesbian scenes, with a gay triangle emerging near the railway line on Leoforos Konstanti-noupoleos and Megalou Alexandrou. In this area, **Blue Train** (📞 210 346 0677; Leoforos Konstantinoupoleos 84, Gazi; Ⓜ Keramikos) is an all-day bar with a club upstairs, and new entrant **8th Sin** (📞 210 347 7048; Megalou Alexandrou 141, Gazi; Ⓜ Keramikos) is stylish and sleek – which could describe the bar or the bartenders!

❻ Hit the Clubs

Venue (📞 210 341 1410; www.venue -club.com; Pireos 130, Rouf; 🕐 Sep-May; Ⓜ Keramikos) lives up to its name. It is arguably the city's biggest dance club with the biggest dance parties by the world's biggest DJs. The three-stage dance floor jumps. Best to cab it late at night.

❼ Winding Down

Down a quiet sidestreet, tiny **A Liar Man** (www.aliarman.gr; Sofroniou 2, Gazi; Ⓜ Keramikos) drips with cool, but has a more hushed vibe. It's the perfect spot for the final nightcap.

PSYRRI

Museum of Islamic Art

Agion Asomaton

Museum of Traditional Pottery **4**

1

Meidani

Thisio

Plateia Thisiou

THISIO

Hill of the Nymphs

200 m
0.1 miles

Paromfilitonos

Melitaiou **5**

Salaminos

Kleomfrotou

Granikou

16 **23**

9

Keramikos

Ermou

Eptahalkou

Akteon

Nileos

Galatas

Erysihthonos

Plateon

Kleomfrotou

Mykinon

Keramikou

Poulen

Iraklidon

Festion

Iera Odos

Piréos

Akteon

Ieralidon

Thessalonikis

Exoneon

Thorikion

Mea Artemisiou

Voutadon

Ierafondon

Technopolis

3 Technopolis

Thisio Park

Vitonos

Evadnis

Dions

Evrymedondos

GAZI

Eirpatridon

Eumolpidon

Iakhou

14

10 ✕

Persefonis

Zakyadon

Iraklidon

Kiriadon

Sfittion

24

Keleou

25 **15**

21 **17**

19 **7**

12

13 ✕

Ikarieon

Keramikos Ⓜ

Gargittion

Dekeleon

Stratoniki

Leof Konstandinoupoleos

Alkiminis

Iera Odos

Rodopis

Grevenon

Leof Konstandinoupoleos

11 ✕

Kreousis

Leof Konstandinoupoleos

Elasidon

8

Piréos

Alkyoneos

20

Volissou

Agi Markellas

Trizinos

Angistis

22

Gefyreon

Paralou

Vasiliou Tou Megalou

Tzaferi

Benaki Museum **2**

Piréos Annexe

Nevrokopiou

Prespas

Emou

Katerinis

Orfeos

Dyaleon

Afidneon

Pittheos

ROUF

Andronikou

18

Votanikos Kipos

VOTANIKOS

Frearion

Plateia Anixeos

6

Sights

Museum of Islamic Art
CULTURAL MUSEUM

1 Map p128, E2

This fine annex of the Benaki museum showcases one of the world's most significant collections of Islamic art. Housed in two restored neoclassical mansions, the museum exhibits more than 8000 items covering the 7th to 19th centuries, including weavings, magic bowls, prayer carpets, jewel-encrusted weapons, ceramics, and a 17th-century reception room from a Cairo mansion. See part of the Themistoklean wall in the basement. A great rooftop cafe overlooks Keramikos and has Acropolis views, but was closed at the time of research. (🗊 210 325 1311; Agion Asomaton 22 & Dipylou 12, Keramikos; adult/child €7/free; ☉9am-5pm Thu-Sun; Ⓜ Thisio)

Benaki Museum Pireos Annexe
ART MUSEUM

2 Map p128, A4

This massive annexe of the Benaki Museum, housed in a former industrial building, helps lead the resurgence in Athens' contemporary visual arts scene. The top-notch modern museum stages massive, well-curated art exhibitions and hosts cultural and historical exhibitions, major international shows, and musical performances in the courtyard. (🗊 210 345 3111; www.benaki.gr; Pireos 138, cnr Andronikou, Rouf;

Technopolis

admission €5; ☉10am-6pm Wed, Thu & Sun, to 10pm Fri & Sat, closed Aug; Ⓜ Keramikos)

Technopolis
CULTURAL CENTRE

3 Map p128, C3

There's always something on at the city's old gasworks, the impressively restored 1862 complex of furnaces and industrial buildings. It hosts multimedia exhibitions, concerts, festivals and special events and has a comfortable cafe. The small **Maria Callas Museum** (🗊 210 346 1589; Technopolis, Pireos 100, Gazi; ☉10am-3pm Mon-Fri; Ⓜ Keramikos) is dedicated to the revered opera diva. (🗊 210 346 7322; Pireos 100, Gazi; Ⓜ Keramikos)

Museum of Traditional Pottery

MUSEUM

4 Map p128, E2

This small museum in a lovely neoclassical building around the corner from the Keramikos site is dedicated to the history of (relatively) contemporary Greek pottery, exhibiting a selection from the museum's 4500-plus piece collection. There's a reconstruction of a traditional potter's workshop. The centre holds periodic exhibitions. (☑210 331 8491; Melidoni 4-6, Keramikos; ⏰9-3pm Mon-Fri, 10am-2pm Sun, closed Aug; Ⓜ Thisio)

Eating

Varoulko

FINE DINING, SEAFOOD €€€

5 Map p128, E1

For a heady Greek dining experience, try the Michelin-starred combination of Acropolis views and delicious seafood by Lefteris Lazarou. The enviable wine list and rooftop terrace help make this one of Athens' big culinary treats. (☑210 522 8400; www.varoulko.gr; Pireos 80, Keramikos; mains €35-60; ⏰from 8.30pm Mon-Sat; Ⓜ Thisio, Keramikos)

Skoufias

TAVERNA €

6 Ⓧ Map p128, A4

This gem of a taverna near the railway line is a little off the beaten track but is worth the cab fare (the area can be sketchy at night). The menu has Cretan influences and an eclectic selection of regional Greek cuisine, including dishes you won't find in any

tourist joint, from superb rooster with ouzo to lamb *tsigariasto* (braised) with *horta* (wild greens). Dine outside at tables opposite a church. (☑210 341 2252; Vasiliou tou Megalou 50, Rouf; mains €4-8; ⏰9pm-late daily, also lunch Sun)

Kanella

TAVERNA €

7 Ⓧ Map p128, B2

Home-made village-style bread, mismatched retro crockery and brown-paper tablecloths set the tone for this trendy, modern taverna serving regional Greek cuisine. Friendly staff serve daily specials such as lemon lamb with potatoes, and an excellent zucchini and avocado salad. (☑210 347 6320; Leoforos Konstantinoupoleos 70, Gazi; dishes €7-10; ⏰1.30pm-late; Ⓜ Keramikos)

Oina Perdamata

TAVERNA €

8 Ⓧ Map p128, B3

Unpretentious, fresh daily specials are the hallmark of this simple spot off busy Pireos street. Try staples like fried cod with garlic dip and roast vegetables, or pork stew, rabbit and rooster. (☑210 341 1461; Vasiliou tou Megalou 10, Gazi; mains €6-9; ⏰noon-midnight; 📶; Ⓜ Keramikos)

Athiri

MODERN GREEK €€

9 Ⓧ Map p128, D2

Athiri's lovely garden courtyard is a verdant surprise in this pocket of Keramikos, while the small but innovative menu playing on Greek regional classics is well executed. Ingredients are sourced from all over Greece and

Museum of Traditional Pottery

combined in fresh, innovative ways.
(📞210 346 2983; www.athirirestaurant.gr;
Plateon 15, Keramikos; mains €16-19; ⏱8pm-
1am Tue-Sat, 6pm-midnight Sun; Ⓜ Thisio)

Sardelles
TAVERNA, SEAFOOD €€

 10 Ⓧ Map p128, C3

Dig into simply cooked seafood
mezedhes at tables outside, opposite the illuminated gasworks. Nice
touches include fishmonger paper
tablecloths and souvenir pots of basil.
Try the grilled *thrapsalo* (squid) and
excellent *taramasalata* (a thick purée
of fish roe, potato, oil and lemon
juice). Meat eaters can venture next
door to its counterpart, Butcher Shop.
(📞210 347 8050; Persefonis 15, Gazi; fish
dishes €10-17; Ⓜ Keramikos)

Jamon
TAPAS €

11 Ⓧ Map p128, B3

Scrumptious tapas and paella are
served streetside with Spanish wines
and flare, by a gregarious owner.
(📞210 346 4120; www.jamon.gr; Elasidon
15, Gazi; tapas €1.75-7; ⏱from 2pm daily;
Ⓜ Keramikos)

Drinking

Hoxton
BAR

12 🍷 Map p128, B2

Join the hip, artsy crowd for shoulder-
to-shoulder hobnobbing amid original
art, iron beams and leather sofas.
(Voutadon 42, Gazi; Ⓜ Keramikos)

Gazaki

BAR

13 Map p128, B3

This Gazi trailblazer opened before the neighbourhood had become *the* place to be. Friendly locals crowd the great rooftop bar. (Triptolemou 31, Gazi; MKeramikos)

45 Moires

BAR

14 Map p128, C2

Go deep into straight-up rock and enjoy superb terrace views of Gazi's neon-lit chimneys and the Acropolis. (Iakhou 18, cnr Voutadon, Gazi; MKeramikos)

Sodade

GAY CLUB

15 Map p128, C2

Athens' premier gay club gets packed with a younger crowd. It's small, but it packs a punch. (210 346 8657; www.sodade.gr; Triptolemou 10, Gazi; MKeramikos)

Nixon Bar

BAR

16 Map p128, D2

More suave than most, Nixon Bar serves up food and cocktails and sits next door to swinging Belafonte. (www.nixon.gr; Agisilaou 61b, Keramikos; MThisio, Keramikos)

Red Dot

BAR

17 Map p128, B2

The newest entry on the Gazi bar scene, the Red Dot has gallery space on lower floors, and a jazz-funk loungey feel both in its music and decor: mural-lined walls leading to an intimate rooftop terrace. (Evmolpidon 24, cnr Triptolemou, Gazi; MKeramikos)

Villa Mercedes

CLUB

18 Map p128, A4

Unashamedly pretentious but undeniably chic. Go for the late-night ultraswanky cocktail and dance scene. It has pleasant outdoor seating, which gets packed, so if you opt to dine, be sure to book ahead. (210 342 2886; www.mercedes-club.gr; Tzaferi 11, cnr Andronikou, Keramikos; MKeramikos)

Noiz Club

LESBIAN CLUB

19 Map p128, B2

Noiz Club is one of the only lesbian bars in Athens and is generally quite straight-friendly. (210 342 4771; www.noizclub.gr; Evmolpidon 41, Gazi; MKeramikos)

Top Tip

Athens' Night Scene

▶ Expect bars to begin filling after 11pm and stay open till late.

▶ Right now, Gazi has the most action, while Kolonaki steadfastly attracts the trendier set and the area around Plateia Karytsi north of Syntagma is up-and-coming.

▶ With the current strapped financial climate in Athens, watch your back, wherever you go.

▶ For the best dancing in summer, cab it to the beach clubs – city locations close.

BIG
GAY BAR

20 Map p128, B1

BIG's a bit out of the way, but it is the hub of Athens' lively bear scene. (www.barbig.gr; Falesias 12, Gazi; ⏱ Tue-Sun; M Keramikos)

S-Cape
GAY CLUB

21 Map p128, B2

This straight-friendly gay and lesbian bar with dancing offers loads of activities. Check the website. (☎ 210 341 1003; www.s-cape-club.blogspot.com; Megalou Alexandrou 139, Gazi; M Keramikos)

K44
CLUB

22 Map p128, B3

K44 hosts a constantly changing schedule of some of the city's hottest parties, bands and DJs, and is frequented by loads of pretty young things. (☎ 210 342 3560; Leoforos Konstantinoupoleos 44, Gazi; M Keramikos)

Entertainment

Bios
CLUB, ART CENTRE

23 Map p128, D2

This avant-garde multifaceted venue popular with an alternative arty crowd has more than just its lively cafe and roof bar with a great view. At times you'll find videos screening, performances on the rooftop, films in the

Top Tip

Gazi Transport
To get to Gazi, definitely take the metro (or cab), which puts you smack in the middle of the scene, and cab it home in the wee hours.

tiny arthouse cinema, live bands and exhibitions in the rambling industrial Bauhaus building. (www.bios.gr; Pireos 84, Keramikos; M Thisio)

Greek Film Archive
CINEMA

24 Map p128, C1

The Greek Film Archive runs occasional international, arthouse film series. Check its website to see if anything's on while you're in town; though it's in English, it sometimes only lists the shows in Greek, when it may be best to call. (Tainiothiki tis Ellados; ☎ 210 360 9695; www.tainiothiki.gr; Iera Odos 48, Gazi; M Keramikos)

Shopping

Rien
CLOTHING, ACCESSORIES

25 Map p128, C1

Penny Vomva designs stylish, sexy clothes with naturalistic lines. Her handbags are supple, colourful leather fancies. (☎ 210 342 0622; www.rien.gr; Triptolemou 2-4, Gazi; ⏱ 4-8pm Wed-Sun, or by appointment; M Keramikos)

The Best of
Athens

Athens' Best Walks

Athens' Best...

Guards outside Greek Parliament (p64)
YADID LEVY/ALAMY ©

Best Walks
Ancient Athens

🏃 The Walk

The key ancient sites of Athens make for an action-packed but manageable walk from the Temple of Olympian Zeus, past the Acropolis Museum and up to the Acropolis, then down around the other side of the hallowed hill into the Plaka and Monastiraki neighbourhoods, where you will find the Ancient Agora and Roman Agora. If you only have one day to see the sights, this is the walk to take.

Start Temple of Olympian Zeus; Ⓜ Akropoli

Finish Ancient Agora; Ⓜ Monastiraki, Thisio

Length 2.4km; three hours

🍴 Take a Break

Two of the easiest spots to stop for a bite to eat or a cool drink are the Acropolis Museum's restaurant, with its magical views of the Parthenon, and **Kuzina** (Map p46, C3; ☏ 210 324 0133; www.kuzina.gr; Adrianou 9, Monastiraki; mains €12-25; Ⓜ Thisio), both are good options on Adrianou for contemporary Greek cuisine.

Theatre of Dionysos (p28)

ATHENS 2004/ALAMY ©

❶ Temple of Olympian Zeus

The **Temple of Olympian Zeus** (p90), the largest temple in Greece, had 104 Corinthian columns, of which 15 remain. It was dedicated to supreme god Zeus. Peisistratos began building it in the 6th century BC, a succession of leaders continued, and Hadrian finally completed it in AD 131.

❷ Hadrian's Arch

Heading towards Plaka, teetering on the edge of the traffic, is **Hadrian's Arch** (p91), the ornate gateway erected in AD 132 to mark the boundary between Hadrian's Athens and the ancient city.

❸ Acropolis Museum

The landmark **Acropolis Museum** (p30) contains the precious sculptures from the Acropolis, preserved in spacious, well-lit glory. These include the caryatids and amazing works from the Parthenon's pediments, metopes and frieze.

4 Ancient Theatres

On the way up the southern slope of the Acropolis, explore the **Theatre of Dionysos** (p28) – the birthplace of theatre – and the magnificent **Odeon of Herodes Atticus** (p29), built in AD 161 and still in use today.

5 Acropolis

The **Acropolis** (p24) is the most important ancient site in the Western world. Take in its diminutive, restored Temple of Athena Nike, then enter through the grand gates of the Propylaia to visit the iconic Parthenon as well as the Erechtheion, with its statuesque Porch of the Caryatids. On a clear day you can see for miles from the sweeping hilltop.

6 Ancient Agora

Exit the Acropolis from the north gate and visit ancient Athens' civic centre: the **Ancient Agora** (p40). The seat of democracy, philosophy and commerce, this rambling site, with the superb Temple of Hephaestus, also has a top-notch museum in the Stoa of Attalos.

7 Roman Agora

The highlight of the **Roman Agora** (p48) is the well-preserved Tower of the Winds. Built in the 1st century BC, it functioned as an ingenious sundial, weather vane, water clock and compass. Each side represents a point of the compass, and has a relief of a figure depicting the wind associated with that point.

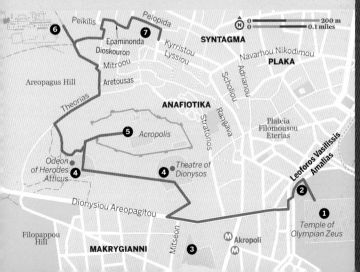

Best Walks
Syntagma & Plaka to Monastiraki

🏃 The Walk

Boisterous, monument-packed central Athens is best explored on foot. The historic centre, as well as the main archaeological sites, major landmarks, museums and attractions, are within a short distance of each other. The main civic hub of Athens, Plateia Syntagmatos, merges into the historic Plaka and Monastiraki neighbourhoods, which mesh one into the next, and make for a super stroll to soak up a bit of city centre life. At any point along the way, ancient sites lie nearby, calling for a detour.

Start Plateia Syntagmatos; Ⓜ Syntagma

Finish Monastiraki Flea Market; Ⓜ Monastiraki

Length 2.5km; three hours

✕ Take a Break

Midway along the walk you can chill out at **Klepsydra** (Map p62, A4; 📞 210 321 4152; Klepsydras, Plaka; snacks €4; 🕐 8.30am-1.30am daily; Ⓜ Monastiraki) cafe, which offers a quiet respite in the busy downtown.

Monastiraki Flea Market (p44)

❶ Plateia Syntagmatos

Start in this **square** (p64) named for the constitution granted on 3 September 1843. Time your visit to catch the changing of the guard outside the parliament building, every hour on the hour. To the left of the metro entrance spot a section of the ancient cemetery and the Peisistratos aqueduct.

❷ Lysikrates Monument

Built in 334 BC, the **Lysikrates Monument** stands in what was once part of the Street of Tripods (modern Tripodon), where winners of ancient dramatic and choral contests dedicated their tripod trophies to Dionysos. Reliefs depict the battle between Dionysos and the Tyrrhenian pirates, whom the god had transformed into dolphins.

❸ Anafiotika Quarter

On Stratonos, which skirts the Acropolis, rises the **Church of St George of the Rock**, which marks the entry to the **Anafiotika quarter**. This picturesque maze of little white-washed houses is the legacy of stonemasons from the small Cycladic island of Anafi, who were brought in to build the king's palace after Independence.

❹ Turkish Baths

Find the **Turkish Baths** (p50) on Kyrristou or inside the free **Museum of Greek Popular Instruments** (p67), which has one of Athens' only remaining private *hammams* in its gift shop.

❺ Plateia Mitropoleos

Jaunt north to expansive **Plateia Mitropoleos**, with **Athens Cathedral** (p48) and its smaller, more historically significant neighbour: 12th-century Church of Agios Eleftherios, known as the **Little Metropolis**.

❻ Hadrian's Library

Pandrosou, a relic of the old Turkish bazaar, is full of souvenir shops and leads to **Hadrian's Library** (p50), once the

most luxurious public building in the city, erected by the eponymous emperor around AD 132.

❼ Monastiraki Flea Market

Wrap up with a wander in Monastiraki. The colourful, chaotic central square teems with street vendors and leads to shopper's or people-watcher's paradise: the **Monastiraki Flea Market** (p44).

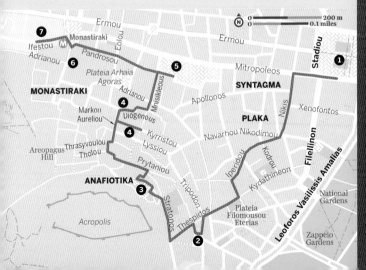

Best
Archaeological Sites

GETTY IMAGES ©

A walk around the archaeological park that is Athens takes in highlights spread over millennia: from the neolithic period to the Classical, Roman and Byzantine eras. In addition to the manmade monuments discussed here, it's worth strolling the promenade up to Filopappou Hill and the Hill of the Pnyx to see ancient terrain and views of the city centre and its shining Acropolis.

Classical Age

The Classical Age (5th to 4th centuries BC) represents the apogee of Greek building. Marble temples (characterised by the famous orders of columns: Doric, Ionic and Corinthian) are epitomosed by the mother of all Doric structures, the 5th-century-BC Parthenon. The Greek theatre is also a hallmark of the classical period. The theatre's cleverly engineered acoustics meant every spectator could hear every word uttered on the stage below.

Roman Athens

The Romans used many of the Greek sites, like the Panathenaic Stadium, adapting them to their needs and occasionally modifying them, or even completing them, as Hadrian did with Temple of Olympian Zeus.

Byzantine & Ottoman Athens

Church-building was particularly expressive during Byzantium in Greece (from around AD 700) and many churches remain, unlike the remarkably few monuments from the four centuries of Ottoman Turkish rule (16th to 19th centuries). Examples of the latter include parts of Plaka, its Fethiye Mosque and the Turkish Baths.

☑ Top Tips

▶ Due to financial difficulties, at the time of writing many sites operated on shorter winter hours (closing around 3pm). This may change.

▶ Be prepared with seasonal gear – sunscreen, hats and water in summer, rain gear in winter.

▶ Bring ID to qualify for student, senior citizen or EU discounts.

Ancient Greek Sites

Acropolis The star of the show, towering over Athens and a thrill to behold. (p24)

Church of Kapnikarea (p50)

Theatre of Dionysos
The birthplace of theatre, on the Acropolis' southern slopes. (p28)

Ancient Agora
Athens' civic, political and commercial centre in ancient times, beautifully preserved. (p40)

Keramikos
The potters' quarter turned cemetery, and ceremonial entrance to Athens. (p124)

Temple of Olympian Zeus
Greece's largest temple, it took over 700 years to build, and was completed by Roman Emperor Hadrian. (p90)

Panathenaic Stadium
Monumental stadium that held ancient contests, Roman sacrifices, and, more recently, the first modern Olympics. (p94)

Roman Sites

Odeon of Herodes Atticus
This magnificent venue on the south slope of the Acropolis is still used for summer festivals, concerts and plays. (p28)

Tower of the Winds & Roman Agora
The civic quarter for the Romans holds the beautifully carved octagonal tower with functions from weather vane to sundial. (p48)

Hadrian's Library
Once the most opulent structure in Athens, erected around AD 132, it had an internal courtyard and pool bordered by 100 columns. (p50)

Hadrian's Arch
The Emperor's monument commemorating the completion of the Temple of Olympian Zeus and marking the border between old and new. (p91)

Byzantine Sites

Church of Agios Eleftherios
From the 12th century, the church incorporates fragments of a classical frieze in Pentelic marble. (p48)

Church of Kapnikarea
The charming 11th-century church sits stranded, smack in the middle of downtown Athens. (p50)

Agios Nikolaos Rangavas
From the 11th century, it was part of the palace of the Rangava family, which included Michael I, emperor of Byzantium. (p61)

Best
Museums

With the embarrassment of riches that is Athens' and Greece's history, museums are superb showcases of all things Greek. On a short visit you'll have to choose among them, but no matter where you go you won't be disappointed.

Archaeological Museums

Many of Greece's most precious statues and artefacts have been collected in Athens for their own protection. In well-lit, temperature-controlled environments these treasures will be able to survive millennia more. The powerhouse is the National Archaeological Museum, the world's best depository of ancient Greek art and artefacts. The Acropolis Museum, opened to much-deserved fanfare in 2009, is a splendid example of showcasing ancient art in a thoroughly innovative, modern setting.

Art Museums

Most of Athens' archaeological museums could equally be characterised as art museums, what with their troves of Greek and Roman sculptures, pottery and jewellery. But the city also has several museums dedicated to more modern forms: painting, etching, contemporary art forms such as installations, and rotating exhibitions of international shows. They also often have educational programs and lecture or music series from time to time.

Cultural Museums

Some museums, particularly in the Plaka and Monastiraki neighbourhoods, focus on more traditional Greek culture. From puppet making to regional dress and musical instruments – pick your poison. The annexes of the Benaki Museum show everything from Greek and Islamic culture to modern art.

THE ART ARCHIVE/ALAMY ©

☑ **Top Tips**

▶ Bring ID to qualify for student, senior citizen or EU discounts.

▶ For the most popular museums, try to go early to beat the crowds.

Archaeological Museums

National Archaeological Museum The world's foremost repository of ancient Greek artefacts in an enormous neoclassical building. (p100)

Acropolis Museum Art and finds from the Acropolis shine in this spacious, superbly curated gem. (p30)

Museum of Cycladic Art Equally an art museum, with minimalist,

Agora Museum, Stoa of Attalos (p41)

ancient Cycladic sculptures that inspired Picasso and Modigliani. (p82)

Ancient Agora Museum Study the history of democracy and Athenian civic life. (p41)

Cultural Museums

Benaki Museum This expansive private collection brings together precious works from all over Greece and the Ottoman Empire. (p76)

Museum of Islamic Art A Benaki annexe housing exquisite examples of Islamic art and culture. (p129)

Kanellopoulos Museum Peruse everything from vases to icons and jewellery in a Plaka mansion. (p64)

Greek Folk Art Museum The main site and its annexes put Greek secular and religious art on show: from embroidery to pottery, weaving and puppets. (p66)

Jewish Museum A small, beautifully displayed collection tracing the history of Greece's Jewish population. (p66)

Art Museums

Benaki Pireos One of the city's leading contemporary powerhouses in a cool converted industrial space. (p129)

Byzantine & Christian Museum Is it art, is it culture? It's simply downright beautiful. (p82)

National Museum of Contemporary Art A loose collection of modern Greek artists with a few international works thrown in for flavour. (p64)

National Art Gallery A rambling collection of predominantly 20th-century art, emphasising Greek painters. (p83)

Theocharakis Foundation for the Fine Arts & Music Rotating exhibitions cycle through this Kolonaki mansion that also offers concert series. (p83)

Best
Food

Traditional Greek cuisine is all about fresh ingredients. Seasonal produce, just-caught seafood, regional ingredients and cooking styles, simple flavours, and minimal dressings bring out the flavours of the Mediterranean. And everything is made tastier by this year's olive oil and a crusty loaf of fresh bread.

GETTY IMAGES ©

Styles of Eateries

Greeks love to eat out and dining is a rowdy, drawn-out communal affair with friends and family. Despite the proliferation of upscale trendy restaurants, the most popular dining venue is the trusty taverna. Most serve a combination of *mayirefta* (oven-baked or casserole-style dishes) and *tis oras* (made-to-order meat and seafood grills).

The mezes-style of dining (usually at a *mezedhopoleio*) is very popular, with small dishes shared over long and merry meals – a variation is the *ouzerie*, where ouzo traditionally helped rinse the palate between mezes tastes.

A *psistaria* is a taverna that specialises in grilled meats with a limited menu of salads and starters.

Souvlaki is still Greece's favourite fast food, both the *gyros* and skewered meat versions wrapped in pitta bread, with tomato, onion and lashings of tzatziki.

Trends

Postmodern tavernas or restaurants (*estiatorio*) with a new generation of classically trained chefs redefine the classics to create modern Greek food. Some add a fusion of styles, from Asia to France; regional cuisine is also prized. Most prominent are fashionable restaurants serving Cretan cuisine.

☑ Top Tips

▶ Greeks eat late (tourist-friendly eateries open earlier). Typically lunch starts around 2pm and dinner 9pm to 10pm; it's not uncommon for tables to start filling at midnight. Tavernas are often open all day.

▶ Athens' seasonal dining scene means many restaurants close for summer, often moving to sister restaurants on the islands or shore.

Best Tavernas

Café Avyssinia A bit like a bistro, with super Acropolis views from upstairs. (p51)

Thanasis (p52) is famous for its souvlaki

Oikeio Top golden ambience, and some international dishes too. (p79)

Kanella Fresh and fab in Gazi. (p130)

Paradosiako Plainly one of Plaka's best. (p68)

Skoufias Way out of the way, but super. (p130)

Best Mezedhes

Tzitzikas & Mermingas Colourful, central and decadent (p67)

Filistron Sweeping Acropolis views from the roof terrace. (p119)

Yiantes In the heart of Exarhia, with savoir faire. (p107)

Filippou Kolonaki's steady best. (p79)

Best Haute Cuisine

Spondi Greco-French top of the tops. (p95)

Varoulko Seafood with flair. (p130)

Mani Mani Regional treats from Mani. (p35)

Hytra Sleek, modern and tasty too. (p51)

Cucina Povera Great wine list and modern, yet still a local feel. (p96)

Best Souvlaki

Kostas Eat standing near the flower market. (p45)

Kalamaki Kolonaki Watch the swank set stroll. (p84)

Thanasis In the heart of Monastiraki's souvlaki strip. (p52)

Best Local

Diporto Agoras Unmarked, down a flight of stairs near the Central Market. (p57)

Kalnterimi Super-fresh home cooking. (p67)

Mama Roux International and all the rage. (p45)

Best Veg-Organic

Avocado From organic all the way to vegan. (p61)

Pure Bliss Lives up to its name. (p69)

Nice N' Easy Has a super weekend brunch. (p85)

Best
Cafes

One Athenian (and Greek) favoured pastime is going for a coffee. Athens' ubiquitous and inevitably packed cafes have Europe's most expensive coffee (between €3 and €5). But with that premium you're essentially hiring the chair, and can linger for hours, watching the cafe action and, alfresco in summer, the passersby. Museums like the Benaki, Acropolis Museum and Theocharakis Foundation also have lovely cafes. And the traditional *kafeneio* (coffee house) can still be found. A *kafeneio* serves Greek coffee, spirits and little else (though in rural villages it may serve food), and remains largely the domain of men.

ANDREW HOLT/ALAMY ©

Best Cafes

Tailor Made Hip new micro-roastery with tea, sandwiches, desserts and a young Athenian crowd. (p45)

Melina Decked out in homage to Melina Mercouri and one of Plaka's few low-key haunts. (p60)

Da Capo The Kolonaki flagship cafe, anchoring the square – it's *the* place to be seen. (p78)

Filion Writers and the intellectual set gravitate here, in Kolonaki. (p85)

Petite Fleur Sweet, like a French cafe, with enormous, steaming capuccinos. (p85)

Kimolia Art Cafe On the edge of Plaka with handpainted tables and an inviting aura. (p70)

Odeon Cafe Mets' corner coffeeshop – a great local hang. (p96)

Vox On the square in Exarhia, live Greek music spices up some weekends. (p109)

Best Teahouses

To Tsai Calming and all-natural, from tea to decor. (p85)

Peonia Herbs On a sidestreet in Thisio with high ceilings and countless brews. (p120)

☑ Top Tip

▶ If you order Greek coffee, it is traditionally brewed in a *briki* (narrow-top pot) and served in a small cup. Let it settle, and then sip it slowly until you reach the muddy grounds at the bottom (don't drink them). It's quite tasty when ordered *metrios* (medium, with one sugar).

Best
With Kids

Hellenic Children's Museum (☎210 331 2995; www.hcm.gr; Kydathineon 14, Plaka; admission free; ⏰10am-2pm Tue-Fri, to 3pm Sat & Sun, closed Jul & Aug; Ⓜ Syntagma) More of a play centre, with a games room and 'exhibits', such as a mock-up of a metro tunnel, for children to explore. Workshops range from baking to bubble-making.

Museum of Greek Children's Art (☎210 331 2621; www.childrensartmuseum.gr; Kodrou 9, Plaka; admission free; ⏰10am-2pm Tue-Sat, 11am-2pm Sun, closed Aug; Ⓜ Syntagma) Has a room where children can let loose their creative energy, or learn about ancient Greece.

Hellenic Cosmos (☎212 254 0000; www.hellenic-cosmos.gr; Pireos 254, Tavros; per show adult/child €5-10/3-8, day pass adult/child €15/12; ⏰9am-4pm Mon-Fri, 10am-3pm Sun, closed 2wks mid-Aug; Kalithea) Take an interactive virtual-reality tour of ancient Greece, about 2km southwest of the city centre.

Planetarium (☎210 946 9600; www.eugenfound.edu.gr; Leoforos Syngrou 387, Palio Faliro; adult/child €6-8/4-5; ⏰5.30-8.30pm Wed-Fri, 10.30am-8.30pm Sat & Sun, closed mid-Jul–late Aug) 3D virtual trips to the galaxy, IMAX movies and other high-tech shows. Narration in English (€1).

Attica Zoological Park (☎210 663 4724; www.atticapark.gr; Yalou, Spata; adult/child €15/11; ⏰9am-sunset) Expanding collection of big cats, birds, reptiles etc. Near the airport. Take bus 319 from Doukissis Plakentias metro station or the shuttle (€5) from Plateia Syntagmatos (see zoo's website).

Allou Fun Park & Kidom (☎210 425 6999; www.allou.gr; cnr Leoforos Kifisou & Petrou Rali, Renti; admission free, rides €2-4; ⏰5pm-1am Mon-Fri, 10am-1am Sat & Sun) Further afield is Allou Fun Park, Athens' biggest amusement park complex. Kidom is aimed at younger children. On weekends they run a bus from Syntagma and the Faliro metro station.

ARIS MESSINIS/AFP/GETTY IMAGES ©

☑ **Top Tips**

▶ The shady National Gardens has a playground, a duck pond and a mini zoo.

▶ There is also a shady playground in the Zappeio Gardens.

▶ Ancient sites make great roaming.

Best
Bars & Clubs

Come nightfall, Athens is undoubtedly one of the liveliest European capitals. A heady cocktail of the hedonistic Greek spirit, restless energy and relaxed drinking laws contribute to the city's vibrant nightlife. The pursuit of a good time is considered almost sacrosanct – as evidenced some years back when moves to impose stricter closing times failed miserably.

BILDERLOUNGE/GETTY IMAGES ©

By Neighbourhood

Athens' sophisticated bar scene includes anything from glamorous bars and hip arty hang-outs to casual neighbourhood haunts. New bars open constantly as fads come and go: a recent hotspot is Gazi, while cool bars are sprouting in the back streets around Plateia Karytsi north of Syntagma and emerging areas like Keramikos. Psyrri goes in and out of fashion. Alternative music clubs and crowded cheap student bars are found around Exarhia, while Kolonaki's scene steadfastly attracts the trendier set.

Party Habits

While mayhem reigns on weekends, weeknights are still surprisingly lively. Bars often don't kick off until 11pm, nightclubs well after midnight, and the city's infamous *bouzoukia* (cabaret-style nightclubs) come alive even later. Most clubs have a door charge and pricey drinks; club-goers dress to impress.

In summer the action moves to rooftop terraces and garden courtyards and spills out onto the pavements, or revellers brave the traffic to party at the beachside clubs.

Athenians don't drink to get drunk (drinks often come with a snack): public drunkenness is uncommon and frowned upon.

☑ Top Tips

▶ With the current strapped financial climate in Athens watch your back wherever you go.

▶ Sky bars, like Galaxy Bar atop the Hilton, offer elevated views (and prices).

▶ For the best dancing in summer, cab it to the beach clubs – city locations close.

Best Classic Drinking Holes

Seven Jokers Central, and great to start the night. (p69)

Hoxton Boho meets celebrity hang-out. (p131)

Mai Tai Jam-packed always...Kolonaki's faithful. (p79)

Rooftop bar overlooking Athens

MAIRA/ALAMY ©

City Anchoring party street Haritos. (p85)

Alexandrino Classic Exarhia wine bar with great cocktails too. (p107)

Tralala A favourite with actors. (p109)

Duende Like a French brasserie. (p36)

Best Specialty Ambience

James Joyce Irish pub attracting expats. (p53)

Blue Fox Rockabilly and '50s-era swing, complete with poodle skirts. (p109)

Brettos Colourful glass bottle-lined distillery. (p70)

Barley Cargo Beer bar galore. (p70)

Galaxy Bar Old-school professionals' bar. (p70)

Second Skin Athens' goth hang-out. (p53)

Booze Cooperativa A collective: from bar to music to crafts. (p70)

A Liar Man Tiny and intimate. (p127)

Best Rooftop Terraces

Gazarte Views from Technopolis to the Acropolis. (p127)

45 Moires Gives Gazarte stiff competition. (p132)

Bios Bauhaus arts centre with great rooftop bar. (p133)

Best Music Bars

Faust Hot, tiny cabaret. (p54)

Ginger Ale Fifties-era coffee shop cum rocking nightspot. (p110)

Best Cocktail Bars

Baba Au Rum Dream it up and they can make it. (p69)

Gin Joint Too many gins to count. (p61)

Bartessera Another great spot in the Syntagma party area. (p69)

Nixon Bar Keramikos' best watering hole. (p132)

Best Clubs

Rock'n'Roll Dependably fun, with a casual-cool crowd. (p79)

Venue Big, thumping mayhem. (p127)

Villa Mercedes Glam dinner-spot and nightclub. (p132)

K44 Rotating schedule of top DJs. (p133)

Best
Nightlife &
Entertainment

Athens has a thriving live-music scene in winter, with the gamut of Greek music from the popular soulful Greek blues (*rembetika*) to jazz, rock and touring international artists. In summer, live music is confined to festivals and outdoor concerts. The full range of symphony, opera and theatre are also on offer.

CARINE VAISSIERE/ALAMY ©

Greek Music & Bouzoukia

Athens has some of the best *rembetika* in intimate, evocative venues. Most close May to September, so in summer try live-music tavernas around Plaka and Psyrri. Performances usually include both *rembetika* and *laïka* (urban popular music), start at around 11.30pm, and do not have a cover charge, though drinks can be expensive.

High-end *bouzoukia* are expensive extravaganzas, like a circus for grown-ups. These glitzy cabaret-style venues (often referred to as *skyladika* – dog houses – because of the crooning singers) are where women dancing the sinewy *tsifteteli* (belly dance) are showered with expensive trays of carnations and revellers party until sunrise. Check listings for what's on.

Cinema & Theatre

An unforgettable Athens experience is a summer's night at one of the outdoor cinemas or theatres. The main summer event is the Hellenic Festival (www.greekfestival.gr; ⏱ late May–Oct), with stagings at the Odeon of Herodes Atticus and other venues.

Best Live Music

Half Note Jazz Club The city's premier jazz venue. (p97)

An Club Eclectic range of acts in Exarhia. (p110)

Cafe Alavastron Many genres in an intimate setting. (p97)

Thission (p121) open-air cinema

Best Rembetika

Stoa Athanaton Legendary club occupying a hall above the central meat market. (p57)

Taximi Loaded on weekends, it's a mainstay. (p111)

Kavouras Above a souvlaki joint in Exarhia. (p110)

Best Music Tavernas

Perivoli Tou Ouranou Old-style taverna with live music in Plaka. (p71)

Palea Plakiotiki Taverna Stamatopoulos Another one of Plaka's busy spots. (p71)

Paliogramofono A Psyrri haunt. (p54)

Best Dance

Dora Stratou Dance Theatre Traditional Greek dances alfresco. (p121)

Best Open-Air Cinemas

Dexameni Kolonaki's sweet cinema, surrounded by gardens. (p79)

Aigli Cinema Zappeio Gardens' fresh-aired spot. (p97)

Thission In Thisio, with Acropolis views. (p121)

Cine Paris Smack in the middle of Plaka, with some Acropolis views. (p71)

> ### Worth A Trip
>
> The city's state-of-the-art concert hall, **Megaron Mousikis** (Athens Concert Hall; ✆210 728 2333; www.megaron.gr; Kokkali 1, cnr Leoforos Vasilissis Sofias, Ilissia; ◷ box office 10am-6pm Mon-Fri, to 2pm Sat; Ⓜ Megaro Mousikis), presents a rich winter program of operas and concerts featuring world-class international and Greek performers. Its Mediterranean-Italian restaurant, Fuga, is home to Michelin-starred chef Andrea Berton.

PIXIDA/ALAMY ©

Best
Gay & Lesbian Athens

For the most part Athens' gay and lesbian scene is relatively low-key, though the Athens Pride (www.athenspride.eu) march, held in June, has been an annual event since 2005, with celebrations centred on Plateia Klafthmonos. For nightlife, a new breed of gay and gay-friendly clubs have opened around town, especially in Gazi, but also in Makrygianni, Psyrri, Metaxourghio and Exarhia.

GEORGIOS MAKKAS/ALAMY ©

Sodade In Gazi; tiny, sleek and super-fun for dancing – it draws a great crowd. (p132)

S-cape Stays packed with the younger crowd and schedules myriad theme nights. (p133)

8th Sin Gazi's newest mod bar spills onto the street. (p127)

Noiz Club Also in Gazi, for women. (p132)

Blue Train Along the railway line in Gazi, has a club upstairs. (p127)

Alekos' Island A veteran establishment, in Psyrri. (p53)

Lamda Club Busy, three levels and not for the faint of heart. (p36)

BIG The hub of Athens' lively bear scene. (p133)

Magaze This gay-friendly all-day hang-out is a cafe by day and becomes a lively bar after sunset. (p52)

Worth a Trip

Mirovolos (☏ 210 522 8806; Giatrakou 12) In Metaxourghio, this cafe-bar-restaurant is a popular lesbian spot. Greek meals range from €16 to €20.

Koukles (☏ 694 755 7443; www.koukles-club.gr; Zan Moreas 32) In Koukaki, the drag show here rocks.

Limanakia This popular gay beach is below the rocky coves near Varkiza. Take the tram or A2/E2 express bus to Glyfada, then take bus 115 or 116 to the Limanakia B stop.

☑ Top Tips

▶ Check out www.athensinfoguide.com, www.gay.gr or a copy of the *Greek Gay Guide* booklet at *periptera* (newspaper kiosks).

▶ Gazi has become Athens' gay and lesbian hub, with a gay triangle emerging near the railway line on Leoforos Konstantinoupoleos and Megalou Alexandrou.

Best
Art Events &
Galleries

ARISTIDIS VAFEIADAKIS/ALAMY ©

Recent years have brought a burgeoning of the arts scene. Even as Athens struggles with other aspects of political or social life, Greece's musicians, performing artists and visual artists remain hard at work and a new breed of multi-use gallery has sprung up to host all of the disciplines. Some feel like museums, others more like nightclubs, and for others it just depends on what time of day it is.

Art Events

Art-Athina (www.art -athina.gr) International contemporary art fair in May.

Athens Biennial (www. athensbiennial.org) Every two years from June to October.

ReMap (www.remap. org) Parallel event to the Biennial, exhibiting in abandoned buildings.

Art Galleries

AD Gallery One of Psyrri's best for contemporary art. (p45)

A.antonopoulou.art Installations, video art and photography by emerging Greek artists in a converted warehouse. (p50)

Qbox Gallery Young, emerging local and visit-ing artists on the international scene. (p57)

Andreas Melas & Helena Papadopoulos Gallery Formerly the AMP Gallery, this new venture merges the efforts of two of Athens' contemporary art powerhouses. (p57)

Xippas Gallery Also has branches in Paris and Geneva. (p79)

CAN The latest for contemporary art. (p84)

Medusa Art Gallery Excellent Greek contemporary painting, sculpture, installations and photography. (p79)

Art Shops

Zoumboulakis Gallery Limited-edition prints and posters by leading Greek artists. (p72)

☑ **Top Tip**

▶ Get a full list of galleries and art spaces at www. athensartmap.net, or pick one up at galleries around town.

El.Marneri Galerie Local modern art and super jewellery. (p36)

Multi-Use Spaces

Taf Exhibitions, bar-cafe, cinema and theatre in interesting crumbling historic building. (p45)

Six DOGS Gregarious – bar, cafe, music venue and theatre. (p45)

Bios Industrial chic with a cinema, a gallery, a bar and more. (p133)

Technopolis City's art complex in the converted gasworks. (p129)

Best
Shopping

Shopping is a favourite Athenian pastime and the number of stores is rather mind-boggling. Major retail development throughout Athens had seen a swath of new stores opening downtown and the city's first major shopping mall launched in the northern suburbs, but the economic problems have reversed that trend.

AEGEAN PHOTO/ALAMY ©

Shopping Districts

The most concentrated high-street shopping is on pedestrianised Ermou, which must have more shoes per square metre than anywhere in the world, as well as most of the leading local, European and global brands. The refurbished Citylink complex houses the Attica department store and is the new gateway to the top international designers and big-name jewellers along Voukourestiou, leading to the chic designer boutiques throughout Kolonaki.

Plaka (with main shopping streets Kydathineon and Adrianou) and Monastiraki (with its enormous flea market) are the places for souvenir hunters, from kitsch statues and leather sandals to jewellery and antiques. Exarhia is the place for more eclectic shoppers, from comics to goth clothing and vinyl. Outlying suburbs Kifisia and Glyfada also offer great shopping, in a more relaxed environment.

Find a delectable array of food and spices at the colourful central market (p57), and all manner of housewares in the surrounding streets.

☑ **Top Tip**

▶ Sale times (July to August and January to February) offer some great bargains.

▶ Haggling is only acceptable (and effective) in smaller, owner-run souvenir and jewellery stores (especially for cash).

Best Food & Drink Shops

To Pantopoleion Full range of Greek goods, near the central market. (p57)

Thymari Tou Strefi Exarhia's go-to shop for local foods. (p111)

Aristokratikon Chocoholics' paradise. (p61)

Mastiha Shop All things made from mastic (the unique sap from Chios). (p61)

Cellier Wine shop extraordinaire. (p72)

Bakaniko Local life in Pangrati: from soup to nuts. (p97)

Best Fashion & Shoes

Parthenis A father-daughter team design in natural fibres and colours. (p79)

Vassilis Zoulias Super-cool couture clothes and shoes with prices to match. (p87)

Ioanna Kourbela Young designer of clothes with flowing lines, in the heart of Plaka. (p61)

Rien Hip Gazi atelier for womenswear and sumptuous leather bags. (p133)

Spiliopoulos Bargain hunters galore come for clothes and accessories. There are three branches. (p55)

Kalogirou Shoe heaven in Kolonaki. (p86)

Melissinos Art Handmade Greek-style leather sandals. (p55)

Best Jewellery

Fanourakis Original, exquisite designs with a minimalist modern bent. Also has a moderately priced line. (p86)

Elena Votsi Contemporary, expensive but oh-so-beautiful. (p87)

Lalaounis Renowned jeweller inspired by Greek history. (p72)

Ikonomou Low-key, and in Plaka, with coral and natural stones. (p61)

Best Cosmetics

Korres Greece's premier organic beauty product company. (p97)

Apivita This natural beauty line in Kolonaki also has an express spa. (p87)

Sabater Hermanos All-natural soaps and bath crystals in Psyrri. (p55)

Best Music Shops

Xylouris Family-run and a font of information on Greek music. (p73)

Vinyl Microstore Vinyl and CDs with a club and indie emphasis. (p105)

Metropolis Music The chain carries a full range from Greek to pop. (p111)

Best Crafts & Antiques

Martinos Selling Greek antiques of all sorts since 1890. (p54)

Aidini Artisanal metal creations from mirrors to candlesticks. (p71)

Goutis Antiques and collectibles from Greece and France. (p87)

Mofu Retro furniture that can be shipped. (p55)

Best Local Shop

Mompso Shop for everything from brass sheep's bells to shepherd's crooks and horse headdresses. (p45)

Best Bazaars

Monastiraki Flea Market A daily extravaganza, not to be missed. (p44)

Athens Central Market Feed your eyes with all the sights at this expansive food market and its surrounding streets. (p57)

Booze Market This occasional craft fair features eclectic, young designers. (p71)

Best
For Free

Best Free Museums

Benaki Museum The top-notch main building (*not* the annexes) is free on Thursdays. (p76)

Kanellopoulos Museum Super cultural museum in the foothills of Plaka. (p64)

Museum of Greek Popular Instruments Displays and recordings of a wide selection of traditional instruments and costumes. (p67)

Museum of Traditional Pottery Lovely neoclassical building near the Keramikos site, dedicated to the history of (relatively) contemporary Greek pottery. (p130)

Epigraphical Museum The most significant collection of Greek inscriptions on a veritable library of stone tablets. (p107)

Maria Callas Museum Dedicated to the revered opera diva: letters, unpublished photos, mementos and videos. (p129)

Best Free to Explore

Filopappou Hill Historic hill strewn with ancient ruins, with some of the best Acropolis views. (p114)

National Gardens Lush sanctuary with a playground and small zoo. (p64)

Best Free Sites

Roman Baths Excavated during the metro build, they are easy to see alongside the National Gardens. (p95)

Syntagma Metro station dig The ancient aqueduct and unearthed artefacts are on display at the metro station. (p138)

Turkish Baths In Plaka, two sites remain, one inside the gift shop of the Museum of Greek Popular Instruments. (p50)

Byzantine Churches All over, they give a glimpse into the heart of Byzantium. (p61)

TERRY HARRIS/ALAMY ©

☑ **Top Tips**

▸ Archaeolgical sites, such as the Acropolis, Temple of Olympian Zeus, Ancient Agora, Roman Agora and Keramikos, are not only included in the €12 Acropolis joint ticket, but are free on all Sundays between November and March. They are free the first Sunday of the month in April, May, June and October.

▸ Sights such as Hadrian's Arch and the Panathenaic Stadium are easy to observe from the street.

Survival Guide

Survival Guide

Before You Go

When to Go

°C/°F **Temp**
40/104 —
30/86 —
20/68 —
10/50 —
0/32 —

Rainfall inches/mm
— 8/200
— 6/150
— 4/100
— 2/50
— 0

J F M A M J J A S O N D

➡ **Summer (Jun-Aug)**
Blazing hot. Accommodation costs most. Athenians leave in August; some restaurants, galleries and bars close. This also applies to Easter.

➡ **Fall (Sep)** Temperatures mild, crowds have thinned. Accommodation prices can drop by 20%.

➡ **Winter (Oct-Mar)**
Temperatures drop; occasional snow. Athens nightlife booms. Accommodation at lowest price. Ferry schedules skeletal.

➡ **Spring (Apr-May)**
Like fall, temperatures are mild; few crowds. Accommodation prices around 20% less than Summer.

Book Your Stay

➡ Plaka is the most popular place for travellers and has a choice of accommodation across the price spectrum. This is the premier sightseeing neighbourhood and is surprisingly quiet at night.

➡ Most of the high-end hotels are around Syntagma.

➡ Some excellent *pensions* and midrange hotels dot the area south of the Acropolis, around the quiet neighbourhood Makrygianni.

➡ Around Omonia some hotels have been upgraded, but there is still a general seediness that detracts from the area, especially at night.

➡ The best rooms in Athens fill up quickly in July and August; book ahead.

➡ Most places offer considerable discounts, especially in the low season, for longer stays and online.

➜ No smoking rules are only occasionally enforced.

➜ For longer stays or if you're travelling with the family, a furnished studio or apartment may offer better value than some of the budget hotels.

Useful Websites

Lonely Planet (www.lonelyplanet.com/greece/athens) Find reviews and book online.

Best Budget

➜ **Hotel Cecil** (www.cecilhotel.gr) Charming old-style hotel with high ceilings and simple rooms.

➜ **Adonis Hotel** (www.hotel-adonis.gr) Friendly staff, tidy rooms and Acropolis-view breakfast room in central Plaka.

➜ **Athens Backpackers** (www.backpackers.gr) From dorm rooms to studio apartments, with a smile and loads of fun.

➜ **AthenStyle** (www.athenstyle.com) Bright, arty hostel with some Acropolis views.

➜ **Hotel Erechtheion** (www.hotelerechthion.gr) Simple and spotless in laid-back Thisio.

➜ **Tempi Hotel** (www.tempihotel.gr) Small, but some rooms have balconies overlooking Agia Irini.

Best Midrange

➜ **Magna Grecia** (www.magnagreciahotel.com) Romantic boutique hotel across from the cathedral.

➜ **Hera Hotel** (www.herahotel.gr) Classic elegance within spitting distance of the Acropolis.

➜ **Athens Gate** (www.athensgate.gr) Dramatic views of Temple of Olympian Zeus at this business hotel.

➜ **Hotel New** (www.yeshotels.gr) Style, style, style at this central design hotel.

➜ **Central Hotel** (www.centralhotel.gr) Sleek rooms in the middle of Plaka.

➜ **Periscope** (www.yeshotels.gr) Mod pods in chic Kolonaki.

➜ **Ochre & Brown** (www.oandbhotel.com) Subtle, suave boutique hotel at the intersection of Psyrri, Monastiraki and Thisio.

Best Top End

➜ **Electra Palace** (www.electrahotels.gr) Plaka's most luxurious, with great food and service to match.

➜ **Hotel Grande Bretagne** (www.grandebretagne.gr) The venerable hotel of royalty and stars, towering over Plateia Syntagmatos.

➜ **Herodion** (www.herodion.gr) Business cool in quiet Makrygianni.

Best Short-Stay Apartments

➜ **Athens Studios** (www.athensstudios.gr) Comfortable, modern apartments near the Acropolis.

➜ **AthenStyle** (www.athenstyle.com) Well-equipped studios; balconies have Acropolis views.

➜ **EP16** (www.ep16.com) Renovated, spacious apartments; the roof garden has Acropolis views. Also apartments in Gazi.

Arriving in Athens

☑ **Top Tip** For the best way to get to your accommodation, see p17.

Eleftherios Venizelos International Airport

➡ Half-hourly blue-line metro trains (one way/return €8/14, one hour) run between the city centre and airport from 5.30am to 11.30pm.

➡ When returning to the airport some trains terminate early at Doukissis Plakentias, where you get out and wait till an airport train (displayed on the train and platform screen) comes along.

➡ Express buses X95 (€5, one to 1½ hours) operate every 15 minutes, 24 hours a day, between the airport and Plateia Syntagmatos, with a few intermediate stops. Buy tickets at the kiosk near the bus stop.

➡ Taxis to the city centre cost €35 (one hour).

➡ Express buses X96 (€5, 1½ hours) operate 24 hours (every 15 to 20 minutes) from the airport to Piraeus, the main port.

Piraeus Port

➡ Metro trains (€1.40, green line) run to the city centre every half-hour from 5.30am to 11.30pm.

➡ Taxis to the city centre cost €30 (45 minutes).

➡ Bus 040 (€1.40) runs to Syntagma every 15 to 20 minutes.

Getting Around

....

Metro

☑ **Best for...**almost all daytime travel; there's an extensive network of conveniently located stations.

➡ The metro (www.amel.gr) runs every three to 10 mins from 5.30am to just after midnight (to 2am Friday and Saturday).

➡ Tickets (€1.40) must be validated at platform entrances and are valid for 90 minutes on all modes of transport.

➡ The three intersecting lines are: green (line 1, also known as the Ilektriko), red (line 2) and blue (line 3).

➡ All stations have wheelchair access.

Taxi

☑ **Best for...**quick trips around town and night-time travel.

➡ Despite the large number of yellow taxis, it can be tricky getting one, especially during rush hour. Thrust your arm out vigorously.

➡ To avoid an argument about the fare, check that the meter is running and set to the correct tariff and expect airport, toll and bag (over 10kg) surcharges. Total fares vary depending on traffic.

➡ If a taxi picks you up while already carrying passengers, the fare is not shared: each person

Transport Maps

Metro maps are quite clear in the stations and onboard trains, but for getting further afield, pick up maps and timetables at the EOT tourist office, the airport and train stations. **Athens Urban Transport Organisation** (OASA; ☏185; www.oasa.gr; Metsovou 15, Exarhia/Mouseio; ⏱6.30am-11.30pm Mon-Fri, 7.30am-10.30pm Sat & Sun), or from its website.

pays the fare on the meter minus any diversions to drop others (note what it's at when you get in).

→ Short trips around Central Athens cost around €5. Beware of taxi scams (p163).

→ Olympic Air offers an online taxi prebooking service.

Taxibeat (https://taxibeat.gr) Mobile app for hailing available taxis by location and rating. Can book from abroad.

Reliable Operators
Booking a radio taxi costs €1.88 extra.

→ **Athina 1** (☎210 921 2800)

→ **Enotita** (☎801 115 1000)

→ **Ikaros** (☎210 515 2800)

→ **Kosmos** (☎18300)

→ **Parthenon** (☎210 532 3000)

Bus & Trolleybus
☑ **Best for...**airport after the metro has stopped running.

→ For the city centre, walking, metro and taxis are almost always the better choice. Buses are better for areas not reached by metro.

→ Athens' overhead cable trolleybuses run between

Tickets & Passes
Tickets good for 90 minutes (€1.40), a 24-hour travel pass (€4) and a weekly ticket (€14) are valid for all forms of public transport except for airport services. Bus/trolleybus-only tickets (€1.20) cannot be used on the metro. Children under six travel free; people under 18 and over 65 pay half-fare. Buy tickets in metro stations or bus booths and at most *periptera* (kiosks). Validate the ticket in the machine as you board your transport of choice.

5am and midnight and service much of the city. Trolleybuses run 24 hours on the 11–Patisia–Pangrati route.

Tram
☑ **Best for...**beach-club hopping.

→ Athens' single tram (www.tramsa.gr) line takes a scenic route along the coast, but it is not the fastest means of transport. It's handy for revellers travelling to the city's beaches and beach clubs (operating around the clock from Friday evening to Sunday, every 40 minutes).

→ The central terminus is opposite the National Gardens. Tickets (€1.40) are purchased on the platforms. Trams run from Syntagma to Faliro (tram 4, 50 minutes) and

to Voula (tram 5, 59 to 65 minutes) from 5am to midnight Monday to Thursday and Sunday and 24 hours Friday and Saturday.

Essential Information

Business Hours
☑ **Top Tip** With the odd economic climate, opening hours and prices are changing continuously; some places close. Call ahead if in doubt.

Standard business hours are as follows, unless specified in the reviews:

Banks 8am to 2.30pm Monday to Thursday, 8am to 2pm Friday

Central Post Offices
7.30am to 8pm Monday to Friday, 7.30am to 2pm Saturday, 9am to 1.30pm Sunday

Bars 8pm to late

Cafes 10am to midnight

Clubs 10pm to late

Restaurants 1pm to 3pm (lunch) and 7pm to 1am (dinner), though most restaurants in central Athens and tourist areas stay open all day in summer.

Shops 9am to 3pm Monday, Wednesday and Saturday, 9am to 2.30pm and 5.30pm to 8.30pm Tuesday, Thursday and Friday (5pm to 8pm in winter). Most major shopping strips in central Athens are open all day; in Plaka and tourist areas, until about 11pm. Department stores and supermarkets 8am to 8pm Monday to Friday, 8am to 6pm Saturday.

Electricity

220V/50Hz

220V/50Hz

Emergency

➡ **Police** (☎100)

➡ **Tourist police** (☎210 920 0724, 24hr 171; Veïkou 43-45, Koukaki; ⏱8am-10pm; Ⓜ Syngrou-Fix)

➡ **Visitor emergency assistance** (☎112) Toll-free 24-hour service in English.

➡ **Ambulance/first-aid advice** (☎166)

➡ **SOS Doctors** (☎210 821 1888, 1016; ⏱24hr) Pay service with English-speaking doctors.

Internet Access

➡ Most hotels and many cafes have internet access or wi-fi.

➡ Free wireless hot spots are at Syntagma, Thisio, Gazi, Plateia Kotzia and the port of Piraeus.

➡ Buy prepaid dial-up internet cards for your laptop at OTE (Greece's main telecommunications carrier) shops or Germanos stores.

Media

English-language papers are the English edition of *Kathimerini*, published daily (except Sunday) with the *International Herald Tribune*, and the weekly *Athens News* and *Athens Plus,* published by *Kathimerini.*

Money

☑ **Top Tip** It's wise to keep cash on hand as many establishments prefer it.

➡ **Currency** Greece uses the euro.

➡ **ATMs** Widely available; usually a charge on withdrawals abroad.

➡ **Credit cards** Accepted in some hotels, restaurants and shops, but certainly not all.

➡ **Money changers** Several around Syntagma, as well as banks.

➡ **Tipping** Small change and rounding up is usually sufficient.

Public Holidays

☑ **Top Tip** Greece's biggest blow-out holiday, Orthodox Easter, is preceded by a week of celebration. The whole country gets a holiday and hotels book up.

All banks and shops and most museums and ancient sites close on public holidays.

New Year's Day 1 January

Epiphany 6 January

First Sunday in Lent February

Greek Independence Day 25 March

Good Friday March/April

Orthodox Easter Sunday 5 May 2013, 20 April 2014, 12 April 2015, 1 May 2016

May Day (Protomagia) 1 May

Whit Monday (Agiou Pnevmatos) 50 days after Easter Sunday

Feast of the Assumption 15 August

Ohi Day 28 October

Christmas Day 25 December

St Stephen's Day 26 December

Safe Travel

➡ Crime has heightened in Athens with the onset of the financial crisis. Though violent street crime remains relatively rare, travellers should be alert on the streets, especially at night, and beware the traps listed here.

➡ Streets surrounding Omonia have become markedly seedier, with an increase in prostitutes and junkies; avoid the area, especially at night.

Pickpockets

Favourite hunting grounds are the metro, particularly the Piraeus–Kifisia line, and crowded streets around Omonia, Athinas and the Monastiraki Flea Market.

Taxi Scams

➡ Most (but not all) rip-offs involve taxis picked up from ranks at the airport, train stations, bus terminals and particularly the port of Piraeus. At

Money-Saving Tips

➡ Look out for free entry at sights (p156).

➡ Buy the one €12 Acropolis ticket (p35) that's good for the six major archaeological sights.

➡ Carry ID for student, EU or senior citizen discounts.

➡ Greek taverna portions are large, and meals are often shared family style – follow this local custom.

Piraeus, avoid the drivers at the port exit asking if you need a taxi; hail one off the street.

➡ Some drivers don't turn on the meter and demand whatever they think they can get away with; others claim you gave them a smaller bill than you did and short-change you. Only negotiate a set fare if you have some idea of the cost.

➡ Some drivers may try to persuade you the hotel you want to go to is full, even if you have a booking.

Bar Scams

➡ Scammers target tourists in central Athens, particularly around Syntagma. One scam goes like this: friendly Greek approaches solo male traveller; friendly Greek reveals that he, too, is from out of town or does the 'I have a cousin in Australia' routine and suggests they go to a bar for a drink. Before they know it women appear, more drinks are ordered and the conman disappears, leaving the traveller to pay an exorbitant bill. Smiles disappear and the atmosphere turns threatening.

➡ Some bars lure intoxicated males with talk of sex and present them with outrageous bills.

➡ Some bars and clubs serve what are locally known as *bombes*, adulterated drinks diluted with cheap illegal imports or methanol-based spirit substitutes. They leave you feeling decidedly low the next day.

Telephone

☑ **Top Tip** In Greece the area code must always be dialled when making a call (ie all Greek phone numbers are 10-digit).

➡ All payphones use OTE phonecards, known as *telekarta* – widely available at *periptera*, corner shops and tourist shops. A local call costs around €0.30 for three minutes. It's also possible to use payphones with a range of discount-card schemes (dial an access code and enter your card number). The OTE version of this is 'Hronokarta'. The cards come with instructions in Greek and English and talk time is enormous compared to standard phonecard rates.

➡ Several mobile service providers offer data and pay-as-you-talk services:

buy a rechargeable SIM card and have your own Greek mobile number. US/Canadian travellers need to have a dual or tri-band system and will have to set their phones to roaming, or buy a local mobile and SIM card.

➡ International access code: 00

➡ Greece country code: 30

➡ International operator: 139

Toilets

➡ Public toilets are a rarity, except at airports and bus and train stations. Cafes are the best option, but you'll be expected to buy something for the privilege.

➡ The Greek plumbing system can't handle toilet paper: the pipes are too narrow. Toilet paper etc should be placed in the small bin next to every toilet.

Tourist Information

EOT (Greek National Tourist Organisation; Map p32; ☎ 210 331 0716, 210 331 0347; www.visitgreece.gr; Dionysiou Areopagitou 18-20, Makrygianni; ⏱ 8am-8pm Mon-Fri, 10am-4pm Sat & Sun

May-Sep, 9am-7pm Mon-Fri Oct-Apr; M Akropoli) The Greek National Tourism Organisation, referred to as EOT, has a free Athens map, public transport information and Athens & Attica booklet. At the time of research, the airport branch was closed.

Athens Information Kiosk - Airport (☎ 210 353 0390; www.breathtakingathens.com; Airport; ⏰ 8am-8pm daily; M Airport) Maps, transport information and all Athens info.

Athens Information Kiosk - Acropolis (Map p32; ⏰ 9am-9pm daily Jun-Aug; M Akropoli)

Travellers with Disabilities

Though some adaptations have been made for wheelchairs, Athens remains a largely inconvenient city for travellers with disabilities. Be specific when booking a hotel to make sure they really can accommodate you.

Visas

EU & Schengen countries No visa required.

Australia, Canada, Israel, Japan, New Zealand & USA No visa required for tourist visits of up to 90 days.

Other countries Check with a Greek embassy or consulate.

Language

Greek is believed to be one of the oldest European languages, with an oral tradition of 4000 years and a written tradition of approximately 3000 years.

The Greek alphabet can look a bit intimidating if you're used to the Roman alphabet, but with a bit of practice you'll start recognising the characters quickly. If you read our pronunciation guides as if they were English, you'll be understood. Stressed syllables are in italics. Note that 'm/f/n' indicates masculine, feminine and neuter forms.

To enhance your trip with a phrasebook, visit **lonelyplanet.com**. Lonely Planet iPhone phrasebooks are available through the Apple App store.

Basics

Hello.

Γειά σας.　　　*ya*·sas (polite)
Γειά σου.　　　*ya*·su (informal)

Good morning/evening.

Καλή μέρα/σπέρα.　ka·*li me*·ra/*spe*·ra

Goodbye.

Αντίο.　　　　an·*di*·o

Yes./No.

Ναι./Όχι.　　　ne/*o*·hi

Please.

Παρακαλώ.　　　pa·ra·ka·*lo*

Thank you.

Ευχαριστώ.　　　ef·ha·ri·*sto*

Sorry.

Συγγνώμη.　　　sigh·*no*·mi

What's your name?

Πώς σας λένε;　　pos sas *le*·ne

My name is ...

Με λένε ...　　　me *le*·ne ...

Do you speak English?

Μιλάτε αγγλικά;　mi·*la*·te an·gli·*ka*

I (don't) understand.

(Δεν) καταλαβαίνω.　(dhen) ka·ta·la·*ve*·no

Eating & Drinking

I'd like ...

Θα ήθελα ...　　tha *i*·the·la ...

a cup of coffee	ένα φλυτζάνι καφέ	*e*·na fli·*dza*·ni ka·*fe*
a table for two	ένα τραπέζι για δύο άτομα	*e*·na tra·*pe*·zi ya *dhi*·o a·to·ma
one beer	μία μπύρα	*mi*·a *bi*·ra

I'm a vegetarian.

Είμαι χορτοφάγος.　*i*·me hor·to·*fa*·ghos

What would you recommend?

Τι θα συνιστούσες;　ti tha si·ni·*stu*·ses

Cheers!

Εις υγείαν!　　　is i·*yi*·an

That was delicious.

Ήταν νοστιμότατο.　*i*·tan no·sti·*mo*·ta·to

Please bring the bill.

Το λογαριασμό, παρακαλώ.　to lo·ghar·ya·*zmo* pa·ra·ka·*lo*

Shopping

I'd like to buy ...

Θέλω ν' αγοράσω ...　*the*·lo na·gho·*ra*·so ...

I'm just looking.

Απλώς κοιτάζω.　ap·*los* ki·*ta*·zo

How much is it?

Πόσο κάνει;　　*po*·so *ka*·ni

It's too expensive.

Είναι πολύ ακριβό.　*i*·ne po·*li* a·*kri*·vo

Can you lower the price?

Μπορείς να	bo·*ris* na
κατεβάσεις	ka·te·*va*·sis
την τιμή;	tin ti·*mi*

Emergencies

Help!

| Βοήθεια! | vo·*i*·thya |

Call a doctor!

| Φωνάξτε ένα | fo·*nak*·ste e·na |
| γιατρό! | yi·a·*tro* |

Call the police!

| Φωνάξτε την | fo·*nak*·ste tin |
| αστυνομία! | a·sti·no·*mi*·a |

There's been an accident.

| Έγινε ατύχημα | ey·i·ne a·*ti*·hi·ma |

I'm ill.

| Είμαι άρρωστος. | *i*·me a·ro·stos |

It hurts here.

| Πονάει εδώ. | po·*na*·i e·dho |

I'm lost

| Έχω χαθεί. | e·kho kha·*thi* |

Time & Numbers

What time is it?

| Τι ώρα είναι; | ti o·ra i·ne |

It's (two o'clock).

| Είναι (δύο η ώρα). | *i*·ne (dhi·o i o·ra) |

yesterday	χθες	hthes
today	σήμερα	si·me·ra
tomorrow	αύριο	av·ri·o
morning	πρωί	pro·i
afternoon	απόγευμα	a·po·yev·ma
evening	βράδυ	vra·dhi

1	ένας/μία	e·nas/*mi*·a (m/f)
	ένα	e·na (n)
2	δύο	*dhi*·o
3	τρεις	tris (m&f)
	τρία	*tri*·a (n)
4	τέσσερεις	te·se·ris (m&f)
	τέσσερα	te·se·ra (n)
5	πέντε	*pen*·de
6	έξη	e·xi
7	επτά	ep·ta
8	οχτώ	oh·to
9	εννέα	e·*ne*·a
10	δέκα	*dhe*·ka

Transport & Directions

Where is ...?

| Πού είναι ...; | pu i·ne ... |

What's the address?

| Ποια είναι η | pia i·ne i |
| διεύθυνση; | dhi·*ef*·thin·si |

Can you show me (on the map)?

| Μπορείς να μου | bo·*ris* na mu |
| δείξεις (στο χάρτη); | *dhik*·sis (sto *khar*·ti) |

I want to go to ...

| Θέλω να πάω | the·lo na *pao* |
| στο/στη ... | sto/sti ... |

Where do I buy a ticket?

| Πού αγοράζω | pu a·gho·*ra*·zo |
| εισιτήριο; | i·si·*ti*·ri·o |

What time does it leave?

| Τι ώρα φεύγει; | ti o·ra *fev*·yi |

Does it stop at ...?

| Σταματάει στο ...; | sta·ma·*ta*·i sto ... |

I'd like to get off at ...

| Θα ήθελα | tha *i*·the·la na |
| να κατεβώ ... | na ka·te·*vo* ... |

Behind the Scenes

Send Us Your Feedback

We love to hear from travellers – your comments help make our books better. We read every word, and we guarantee that your feedback goes straight to the authors. Visit **lonelyplanet.com/contact** to submit your updates and suggestions.

Note: We may edit, reproduce and incorporate your comments in Lonely Planet products such as guidebooks, websites and digital products, so let us know if you don't want your comments reproduced or your name acknowledged. For a copy of our privacy policy visit lonelyplanet.com/privacy.

Our Readers

Many thanks to the travellers who used the last edition and wrote to us with helpful hints, useful advice and interesting anecdotes: Jay Lee, Viktoria Urbanek.

Alexis' Thanks

As always, hail Alexandra Stamopoulou for her spot-on recommendations and unflagging friendship. Mihalis Pelekanos generously shared his top eating and nightlife tips, and Cathryn Drake her art scene expertise. Thanks to Stefanos Hatzopoulos for his architectural acumen and Ilias Nikolaidis for super suggestions. Margarita Kontzia, Kostas Karakatsanis and Anthy and Costas made Athens home and always shared their superlative knowledge of the city.

Acknowledgments

Cover photograph: Caryatids of Erechtheion at the Acropolis/George Tsafos/Lonely Planet Images©.

This Book

This 2nd edition of Lonely Planet's *Pocket Athens* guidebook was researched and written by Alexis Averbuck. The previous incarnation, *Athens Encounter*, was written by Victoria Kyriakopoulos. This guidebook was commissioned in Lonely Planet's London office, and produced by the following:

Commissioning Editor Katie O'Connell **Coordinating Editors** Andrea Dobbin, Ross Taylor **Coordinating Cartographer** Xavier Di Toro **Coordinating Layout Designer** Carlos Solarte **Managing Editor** Brigitte Ellemor **Senior Editors** Andi Jones, Susan Paterson **Managing Cartographers** Shahara Ahmed, Mandy Sierp **Managing Layout Designer** Chris Girdler **Cover**

Research Naomi Parker **Internal Image Research** Barbara Di Castro, Claire Gibson **Language Content** Samantha Forge **Thanks to** Dan Austin, Anita Banh, Gordon Christie, Ryan Evans, Jouve India, Asha Ioculari, Trent Paton, Anthony Phelan, Raphael Richards, Averil Robertson, Fiona Siseman, Andrew Stapleton, Rob Townsend, Diana Von Holdt, Gerard Walker

Index

See also separate subindexes for:

⊗ **Eating p173**

◔ **Drinking p174**

✪ **Entertainment p175**

🔒 **Shopping p175**

🍴 Eating

Our Writer

Alexis Averbuck

Alexis lives on Hydra, Greece, and takes regular reverse R&R in Athens to get a dose of city life. Always thrilled to explore the best-kept secrets of her adopted land, she is committed to dispelling the stereotype that Greece is simply a string of sandy beaches. Whether people-watching in Athens' busy cafes or tripping the light fantastic with her Athenian friends, she enjoys getting to know each of Athens' distinct neighbourhoods and finding its latest surprises.

A travel writer for two decades, Alexis has lived in Antarctica for a year, crossed the Pacific by sailboat and written books on her journeys through Asia and the Americas. She's also a painter – to see her work visit www.alexisaverbuck.com. Read more about Alexis at www.lonelyplanet.com/members/alexisaverbuck.

Published by Lonely Planet Publications Pty Ltd
ABN 36 005 607 983
2nd edition – Jan 2013
ISBN 978 1 74179 707 7
© Lonely Planet 2013 Photographs © as indicated 2013
10 9 8 7 6 5 4 3 2 1
Printed in China